Transnational Taiwan

David Pendery

Transnational Taiwan

Crossing Borders into the 21st Century

palgrave
macmillan

David Pendery
National Taipei University of Business
Taipei, Taiwan

ISBN 978-981-19-4367-6 ISBN 978-981-19-4368-3 (eBook)
https://doi.org/10.1007/978-981-19-4368-3

This Palgrave Macmillan imprint is published by the registered company Springer Nature Singapore Pte Ltd.
The registered company address is: 152 Beach Road, #21-01/04 Gateway East, Singapore 189721, Singapore

This book is dedicated, as always, to my mother, wife, and daughter.

And in remembrance of my father, Donald Bruce Pendery (1932–1976), who gave me intellectual curiosity.

This work, as my other Taiwan studies, is also for the people of Taiwan.

Preface

I did not plan to write this foreword, but when a scholar I know promised, and then refused to do so, it became necessary. I will not go into great detail about our topic here—Taiwan's (and the world's) transnational character—as I will go into that in detail in the pages that follow. To approach it simply, this is a highly important topic in today's global ecosystem, the international relations that we are so fully involved in, with Taiwan's prickly position therein always at the forefront of any analyses. Whether Taiwan can be taken into this context "transnationally" (that is, "nationally") at all, is, to say the least, an open question—not least because of China's obstinate, often reckless obstruction (I use a less-than-combative description). I have considered just this question often in my books, editorials, and comments. Without probing into yet more detail here, the simple question remains: To what extent can Taiwan be considered "transnational" in international conceptions and contexts today? Given my previous commentary, I need hardly to say further that Taiwan can be considered just this. This "nation," with all of its rich history (political, economic, social, etc.), linguistic diversity and peoples (not least indigenous), varied cultures and interlopers of all kinds within its borders, unique geography, interaction in world trade, its own laws, customs, norms, identity, and a functioning government—is in more than a sturdy position to be seen as very much, very opulently, very amply, "transnational," whatever gripes and censure come from the "other side" of this discussion. And that probably says it all, and introduces just how we will enter into, discuss, analyze, and wholly embrace this subject. That which is transnational has become that which is wholly ***that which is*** life, polity, community, and yes, "state" in today's international environment and setting. And so, let's explore how Taiwan (and a good bit of the rest of the world) fits into just this milieu. The transnational time is now, let's embrace it for all it is worth, for all it has to offer, in Taiwan and all around the world.

Taipei, Taiwan David Pendery

Contents

About the Author

David Pendery was born in Cincinnati, Ohio in 1960. He relocated with his family to Albuquerque, New Mexico at the age of nine, and grew up there. He moved to San Francisco in 1984, and obtained a B.A. in International Relations at San Francisco State University, and later an M.S. in Journalism at Boston University. He lived and worked as a technician and writer in these cities until 2000, when he relocated to Taipei, Taiwan. Here he has worked as an English consultant, teacher, journalist, and editor. He obtained his Ph.D. in English literature and historiography at National Chengchi University in Taipei. He is currently an associate professor in the Department of Applied Foreign Languages at National Taipei University of Business. He is married to a Taiwanese woman, and they have a six-year-old daughter.

CHAPTER 1

Transnationalism: An Overview and a Look at Taiwan

Abstract This work is a review of transnationalism at the high level, and an introductory look at Taiwan's transnational fabric. It includes a look at the definitional terms "international" and "transnational," with additional looks at "simu-," "socio," and "accord" usages. There is a continued look at transnational, and a first indication of historical realities. Following is an introduction of Randolph Bourne, and the first use of transnational in analysis. There is a look at geography and transnationalism, and an introduction of the "challenge to the nation state" in these terms. There is an introduction of deterritorialization, homogenization, assimilation, borders and control. It will include the first mention of "newlands," and a look at how travels and migrations can be broadly interpreted as flows of ideas, discourse and cultural artifacts. There is an introduction of "social fields," and an examination of transnationalism, as an economic concept, and a look at globalization as a less-than-ideal conception in these terms. The chapter includes a look at NGOs and their importance in these terms, and a look at other sources and drivers of transnationalism.

Keywords Transnationalism · Taiwan · Migration · Geography · Diaspora · Randolph Bourne · NGOs · Definitions

D. Pendery, *Transnational Taiwan*,
https://doi.org/10.1007/978-981-19-4368-3_1

The conception of the transnational state is, at the highest level, "economic, political, and cultural processes that extend beyond the boundaries of nation-states" (*Britannica*), and in turn "Cross-border circulations of people and ideas..." driven by "...advances in transportation and communication, diffusion of technology and ideologies, large-scale movements of capital, labor, tourists, commodities, and culture artifacts, expansion of mass education, creation of transnational public spheres and institutions and relocation of production facilities 'abroad'" (Hau 1). This all takes place in a field that will be reexamined often in this work, "both locally and internationally, in the new host nation and the country of origin" (Adachi 9).

In this analysis, I will put Taiwan into extended transnational contexts and foci, with the aim of understanding this conception, and highlighting processes and relationships that transcend nation-states and seek to connect ostensibly separate peoples, worldviews, regions, and identities in this nation. I will examine how Taiwan has achieved a transnational status globally in terms of the experiences of the diverse, international populations from all nations that live, work, and are educated here, its open governmental structures and processes, its own history (which has had numerous transnational takes and developments, including Taiwanese diasporas, which have been occurring since time immemorial), Taiwanese indigenous peoples (who themselves have their own unique views of these routes and developments), business and working conditions, conflict and security in this new world, students and education, and the notion of transnational subjectivity, which is present in all the people who live in Taiwan, whether native or foreign, and imbues them with a transnational/international view onto existence, taking in peoples of every type. In sum, transnational understanding in Taiwan suggests not only a historical understanding of the movements and interactions of peoples, but also a move "beyond a national framework of analysis, to explore connections between peoples, societies and events usually thought of as distinct and separate" (Heylen 12).

Even here we must pause, however, and ask about the meaning of "transnational" proper, compared to the probably more common understanding of "international." "Trans-" of course, simply means "across," and thus this idea means "across nations" ("across borders" is probably the more common understanding in the terms we are addressing). "Inter" means "among, between," and thus we see in this idea interactivity, collaboration and communication among nations. I am inclined to doubt whether there is much difference at all between these two denominations, and transnational appears to have become popular because analysts (you actually don't, hear many ordinary people use the term "transnational") like the idea of travels across borders, and the broad range of possible entities doing this—migrants, immigrants, travelers, tourists, aliens, expatriates, evacuees, exiles, refugees, nomads—as opposed to simply nations—politicos and citizens in action, associating with one another. We may find ourselves sometimes referring to that which is "international" as opposed to "transnational" in this analysis, but that seems a reasonable outcome, and will not detract from our examination.[1]

As well, I am inclined to think that that which is *transnational* might be understood as *simu-*, *socio-* or *accordo*-national, and I rather like these conceptions, the first indicating that which is simultaneous, in the same offing, the second a given sociality, and the third that which is in accord, shared. Others, however, might defer, preferring to maintain the essential idea of crossing borders. Note here that that which is "national" and the "nation" proper maintains validity, in the terms outlined by Willis, which is to say that the nation, even in changeful modern conditions, with such extensive mobility at work in terms of people coming and going, retains an importance and value for travelers, citizens, migrants, etc. The fact that nations themselves do have certain valued qualities, and have much to offer these people politically, socially, economically, etc., must be taken into account (see Willis's analysis, below). I am in part in support of this view. In any event, now and going forward, we will continue to view and analyze the *transnational*, with all it has to offer.

As an aside, in all of the above, we may see how transnationalism extends beyond expected norms, and "belies constructed national boundaries by *operating within, but not because of*, their imagined parameters" and that we may need to employ "an imagination capable of articulating an integrated world of multiple modernities, and a language that can accommodate, even facilitate difference" (Heylen 29, italics in original).

[1] Readers might be interested to know that Jürgen Habermas has referred to a "postnational constellation" in terms of all we are examining (Jürgen Habermas, *The Postnational Constellation*, 2001).

The transnational conception appears to be a relatively new conception in global affairs, but it is not actually that. Transnationalism, as noted, has been defined as the extension across national borders of:

- Peoples and cultures
- Capital and flows of money
- Goods and technology
- Social and cultural ideas and practices.

Simply put, this is a concept looking at networks of influence and connections that overtop the nation, proper—and this is something we have been seeing for centuries (and much more on transnationalism as a continuing and veritably ancient topic, not least in terms of Taiwan, below). See how such allowances "include immigration, migration and business and tourist travel of peoples" (*Thoughtco*), yielding new networked communities comprised of, to repeat, migrants, immigrants, travelers, tourists, aliens, expatriates, evacuees, refugees, exiles, and nomads. In a word, we live in a new (but then again, not) world of "global interconnectedness," in which "people on the move are able to sustain and extend social life into widespread networks of relations including both source and destination countries" (Sørensen 6). The "state" has not disappeared, as some activists have hoped, but it is taking on a new definition within this interconnected world (and much more on this idea, below).

The transnational conception appears to have originated in the early twentieth century, popularized by American Randolph Bourne, a progressive writer and radical during World War I—but it is vital to be aware that this was not an unknown concept in prior ages. Bourne described a nominally new way of thinking about relationships between cultures, recognizing "the uniqueness of this trans-nationalism of ours" (Bourne, no page number). This nominal nationalism would go beyond the "hyphenates" (as we say in the United States) and "weave a wholly novel international nation" (Bourne). Bourne endorsed this new conception, a new "hope and promise" (Bourne), with concern about the looming World War I in Europe. A transnationality of all nations was arising (due to World War I most likely, and in a large sense, European people at this time were the first who actually began to see the world this way), and there was an "attempt to weave a wholly novel international nation out of our chaotic America [in order to] liberate and harmonize the creative power of all these peoples and give them the new spiritual citizenship, as so many individuals have already been given, of a world" (Bourne). All of this is now being taken up in the twenty-first century, and this "new" movement now focuses on a heightened interconnectivity between nations and peoples, along with a declining economic and social significance of borders and state sovereignty.

Transnationalism is seen as a force that is rethinking the role of geography, nationhood, and residency in the formation of identity.[2] And here, we might pause to examine a common perception of geography in the modern world. This is that it is seen that transnationalism, proper, has introduced the "death of the nation-state" into politics and international affairs, a "challenge to the continued existence of the 'nation,' or more often, the 'nation-state'" (Willis et al. in Yeoh 1).

Robinson writes further that "Social structure is becoming transnationalized, and an epistemological shift is required," a change "predicated on a paradigmatic shift in the focus of social inquiry from the nation-state as the basic unit of analysis to the [transnational] global system" (561, with added wording). He goes on that "interactive networks" of migrating peoples "operate both 'over' and 'under' the nation state system, and undermine its institutional logic and any rationality in conceiving of social structure in national terms" (567). "Economic and political networks," he goes on, "are increasingly located in transnational space and managed by transnational classes and groups that exhibit conflict among themselves not correlative with nation-state or territorial dynamics" (570). All of this "underscores the highly contradictory nature of transnational relations as well as the indeterminacy of emergent transitional social structure" (581). In many respects, Robinson follows a fairly standard globalized economy/system argument in his analysis, but we see his shift from a focus on the nation-state, and will see a good measure of equivocal "borderlessness" in the following.

[2] Edward W. Said (1935–2003) calls the conception of identity a set of geographically based "structures of attitudes and reference" (53), by way of which "the new economic and socio-political dislocations and configurations of our time" (330) must be matched and accorded with "the startling realities of human interdependence on a world scale" in the modern day (220). Geography is, in a word, "about ideas, about forms, about images and imaginings" (7).

We may be seeing "limitations of the nation state as a collective agent, as a geopolitical, economic, cultural system" (Hau 1). The "volume of flows" of migrants and all they bring with them, "have eroded the sovereignty and capabilities of the nation-state, rendering its borders far more permeable…and opening it to the world far beyond the reaches and control of the territorially rooted state" (Hau 1).

None other than Henry Kissinger has considered the decline of the nation-state, although not in the terms we are considering, in his *World Order* (2014). Ever the hard-nosed realist theoretician (you'll find no notion of a more open transnationalism in his work), Kissinger, principally looking at the essential failure of some Islamic states in the modern era (Syria, Iraq, failings in Saudi Arabia, and Iran), comments on "the disintegration of statehood into tribal and sectarian units, some of the cutting across existing borders" (142). Some might ask if transnational re-groupings and the given flexibility of state borders in the new age are somehow similar. These "states" (they are hardly that any more) "may prove unwilling or unable to reestablish authority over border regions or non-state entities" (142), and the same doubts may arise in some people's minds. "When states are not governed in their entirety," Kissinger writes, "the international or regional order…begins to disintegrate. Blank spaces denoting lawlessness come to dominate parts of the map…Political, sectarian, tribal, territorial, ideological and traditional national-interest disputes merge" (143–144). To what extent transnationally relocated citizens of the world can be seen in such terms appears very doubtful to this writer, but the basic idea may be considered (and we will see more below when we examine "Transnational Conflict, Security and Militarization"). Kissinger further notes that "Participants in [such contests] search for outside support" (144), which we will see Samuel P. Huntington repeat below (we may well view Huntington and Kissinger in the same light). Needless to say, all of this is a major threat to decent world order, but to step back, we believe that with transnational attitudes, activities, and behaviors, we are more likely to see a given *reordering of world order* (in other words, *not* a disintegration), into potentially a "new regional order" (Kissinger 145), which although not a given, does imply something better.

To return to our principal analysis (and to avoid the negativity of Kissinger), although it is true that we see a number of limitations being imposed on the nation-state in the present day, the central idea of the state's decline and disintegration is a stretch, for the very idea of the "nation" is impounded into the idea of the "transnational." Willis et al. point out that "the continued importance of the 'nation-state' is a key feature distinguishing transnationalism for the supposedly more deterritorialized concept of 'globalization'" (in Yeoh 1), and that the very idea of "crossing borders" indicates this. "The concept of transnationalism only has meaning in a world divided into nation-states," as Stephen Castles puts it (in Yeoh 16). Castles continues that a "core feature of the classical nation-state is its claim to manage ethnic difference—through border control, as well as through processes of cultural homogenization [assimilation might be a better description] or subordination of minorities" (Yeoh 16). This is a bit clear of what we are actually looking at, but these ideas of homogenization, assimilation, borders, and control are applicable in our study, and can be seen as indications of the processes and experiences that migrants and other travelers are faced with. This is a fair view, and although the idea of the "death of the nation state" will reappear in this text (and has particular relevance in terms of Taiwan), it is perhaps important that we not go quite so far, and give the nations and their citizens/peoples their due in terms of transnational activity (travels and migrations), and subjectivity (and much more on this below).[3] This might be to say that we go "beyond a national framework of analysis, to explore connections between peoples, societies and events usually thought of as distinct and separate" (Heylen 12). In any event, we will very much see these ideas, conceptions, and limitations applied to the Taiwan experience throughout this work. Many such peoples, and the entities they are interacting with (notably international businesses we might say), still very much feel certain attachments to, and the necessity of, "nation states" with their "borders." That they are "trans-ing" across these fields does not truly diminish their importance. Let us keep this idea in mind as we move forward, however much we do the "trans-" thing across nations, states, and borders.

Rather than viewing migrants as simply agents who move between bounded and separate worlds, modern geographers have been interested

[3] Note in the above how travels and migrations can be broadly interpreted as flows of ideas and discourse enabled by inflows of not just goods and commodities, but an entire range of cultural artifacts, including books, films, presences on the Internet, varieties of made and constructed objects, art works, representations, iconography, memes, "mentifacts" (cultural traits taken in as single identifiable materials or elements, and conceivable as objects; from Wikipedia, "Cultural Trait"), iconography, and finally, as noted above, subjectivity.

in how migrants' social spheres may be conceived as "the same society differentially located in space but tightly woven across borders" (Huang, no page number). Given "social fields" do not necessarily coincide with the territorial space of the nation-state. It is in these transnational social spaces, or trans-localities (a sort of living in more than one place at a time) where the everyday activities and geographies of transnational communities occur, accumulate, and transact, enabling (re-enabling we might say) trans-migrants, who share forms of identity within dense networks of social relations in host societies (newlands we will call them). As well, we see the creation and maintenance of links with home and other trans-local spaces in other parts of the world, all taking place in a multidirectional manner. These social spaces may be immaterial entities, such as business networks, but they also include real geographic spaces, whether formally construed, as in social clubs and expatriate organizations, or informally convened, such as in migrant contract workers' weekend enclaves and life within their own communities. These networks and social locations can importantly influence transnational adaptation and flows across transnational spaces, and in turn arbitrate flows of information, finance, commodities, communitarian ideas, and cultural/social values. Traditionally bounded ideas of community and locality based on fixed spaces are thus superseded by a "relationally constituted sense of 'citizenship'" or simply the conception of "being a local," can arise (Huang, no page number).

To refer at length to Huang, slightly modified, in the above terms, the boundaries of social fields do not necessarily coincide with the territorial space of the nation-state. We will see often in this work how this applies to the Taiwanese experience. In these transnational social spaces, the everyday activities and geographies of transnational communities transpire, and accrue meaning and connotation for transnational arrivals. This enables transnationals in newlands (many who share distinct qualities and mutual forms of identity, while still very much retaining connections to their homelands) to find and develop dense networks of social relations, while maintaining multidirectional links with other transnational spaces in other parts of the world.[4]

Transnationalism, as an economic concept, stems from the fact that borderless new economic interactions are taking place worldwide,

[4] At one level Said defines these associations, sometimes-conflicts and links as a "contrapuntal analysis," in which various "intertwined and overlapping histories" (18), and

combining the reorganization of production processes within stages of actual production occurring in various localities or countries. Consequently, changes in the global economic order are occurring, including the rise of developing economic powers, citizen and government attention to economic injustice, and the distribution of global wealth (and associated asymmetrical power relations), waves of migrant workers entering new countries, the emergence of China as an economic powerhouse, and, at the highest level, the emergence of a new multi-polar world order in which any number of nations have new economic precedence and standing. Again, in terms of economy, Taiwan very much comes into play, with its booming economy and technological prowess attracting visitors and workers from around the world, often to live here for extended periods. More on this below.

Economic transnationalism is perhaps commonly known as globalization, which is to be sure central to the overall approach, but as an essentially economic concept, does not go far enough. Globalization is too "neat," a catchword that does not really make sense, either empirically or experientially. Organizations, activities and individuals now arc across assorted discrete levels, rendering obsolete these prior lines of discrimination. In the transnational world, "the actors may now be individuals, groups, movements, business enterprises, and, in no small part, it is the diversity of organization which we need to consider" (Hannerz in Djelic 140). Multinational corporations (MNCs), economic giants to be sure, will be important in this analysis, and have introduced their own brand of transnationalism. They are organizing their operations in what is hoped will be the efficient means, irrespective of political boundaries, and in turn they are participating in and in some senses initiating new legal frameworks. But again, this not the complete picture. In this analysis, we will go well beyond a strictly liberal/capitalists breed of transnationalism, and seek to investigate cultural, political, and identity-focused issues of this topic. Though Taiwan is itself home to a number of major MNCs, and often touts itself as an economic powerhouse in the throes of globalization, we will in turn see foci on these just-mentioned issues, not least in terms of what several Taiwanese commentators and students have to say in this analysis.

"discrepant experiences" (32) must be seen alongside one another, with a reading considering how they impact and influence each other as a "system of relationships, all of them coexisting and interacting" (Said, 32, slightly reworded).

Broadly in terms of the above, let me focus on one aspect—the idea of nongovernmental organizations (NGOs) in terms of our subject (I am referring in some senses to the MNCs noted above, which though not usually thought of as NGOs proper, can be seen in such a light; I am thus broadening the topic a bit, but allow me that). Taiwan's unofficial or nongovernmental relations with various entities may be most essential in the transnational ways we are discussing, and they thus take on a greater importance when compared with official diplomatic recognition, which is no doubt a hot topic in Taiwan at all times. And to be sure Taiwan is active in these areas, with work with NGOs providing funding and cooperative work in areas of agriculture; medicine and public health; education; transportation, logistics and construction; "people to people" communications; women's rights; environmental protection; humanitarian assistance and disaster relief; and technical development. In this respect, what Taiwan may need, transnationally, are capacious ongoing relations with various organizations and institutions—dubbed unofficial or nongovernmental—instead of existing state-to-state interactions. Given that many of the groups indicated here are enormously important and influential, such relationships can foster an elevated level of reciprocity, trustworthiness, credibility, mutual validity and legality, which are no doubt of critical importance and could be beneficial to Taiwan, leading to even better outcomes (Amnesty International, Doctors Without Borders, Save the Children, the Library Project, Human Rights Watch, Greenpeace, the World Health Organization, Reporters Without Borders, and the Committee on Space Research are among the main organizations that might be involved; Taiwan has substantive connections with some of these entities).[5] When I refer here to reciprocity, trustworthiness, credibility, mutual validity and legality, we are led toward a transnational understanding of civic affairs and politics (as well as cooperative effort and international law). In a word, these connections may fall short of diplomacy proper, but they can have a real impact on transnational arbitration. This sounds a bit like "governance," which I will explore in detail below.

[5] In terms of the World Health Organization, Taiwan has had semi-substantive relations, but these have largely come to a halt due to Chinese interference. Presently, the nation is seeking to join the WHO's World Health Assembly decision-making body as an observer, with little success to date. In 2021, however, 163 events were held in various locations worldwide, "calling for Taiwan's participation in the World Health Assembly, with participation from 800 organizations and 17,055 people" (Chen Yu-fu, *Taipei Times*).

We have witnessed a considerable increase in the number and importance of NGOs, as well as the prominence of their output, capabilities, and functions. Betsill and Corell write that we must "perceive the participation of NGOs as an efficient equivalent of delegation by the state" (in Biedermann 30). Their incorporation into civil structures, and their connection to governmental systems, has indicated their growing importance in the formulation of national and international policy. The environment in which these groups function has proven to be stable and favorable for accomplishment of diverse objectives, and functions and activities have been formulated with transparent, accountable mechanisms employed in necessary decision-making. NGOs are doing much more than simply observing from the sidelines and have become vital to developing and implementing policies and processes. Many of them are financially self-sufficient and capable of creating and conducting their own programs and agendas, with substantial autonomy in relation to states. Here again are hints of, and the out-and-out existence of, transnational realities.

To continue, different views have focused on other sources and drivers of transnationalism. Some analysts argue that the main driver of transnationalism has been the development of technologies that have made transportation and communication more accessible and affordable, thus changing relationships between people and places (this will again be connected with globalization, which I am avoiding). The Internet and social networking have made it more possible for immigrants to maintain closer contact with their home societies than was once true. We will see often in the following that such connections to homelands are very much part of the overall transnational picture. In any case, Taiwan as a driver and center of technological development, and its very advanced transportation systems, can be seen as important in these lights. In some respects, such developments can be viewed as "local," simply aspects of Taiwanese economic entities, citizenry, and governance, emerging out of the efforts of the people of Taiwan in the here and now; but this does not mitigate their importance when being used by the transnational peoples who make Taiwan their home.

The very idea of "migration" gives rise to the related notion of the diaspora—those migrants, most of them related culturally and linguistically, traveling together, or traveling apart and then finding themselves near one another in given newlands (much more on migration and diasporas below). This conception of diaspora, however, is perhaps a bit more complex than it appears on its surface. "Most diasporas are internally differentiated," writes Sorensen (200), and "links between the different social layers within a diaspora must exist" (200). Given "contexts" shape diaspora formations, including the just-mentioned internal divisions; conceptions of community, activism, and elitism; active links with home countries and the degree to which home governments encourage varied new linkages; monetary and social remittances; rights and privileges in newlands; and the reality that "organized diaspora groups are representative of broader development goals encompassing the transnational social field of home country interests" (all from Sorensen 200–201).

Needless to say, instances of diasporas are manifold worldwide—I need hardly note the Jewish diaspora, European, African, and Asian diasporas (notably that of the Chinese people, to be looked at again below), eras of colonialism and post-colonialism, and to some extent changes in population after the fall of the USSR. I am also inclined to mention the travels of the Siberian peoples across the Bering Strait up to 30,000 years ago, and their move into the Americas—a truly transnational move that long ago! Taiwan has itself experienced diasporas of its own—and below I will look at the "Out of Taiwan" thesis, which postulates a given movement of masses in ancient times out of Taiwan, and into the wider Indo-Pacific and Austronesian regions. Further, I will look at diasporic Taiwan in the modern day.

At the highest level, although the transnational conception is seen as "new," veritably twenty-first century, this is by no means the case. For in fact transnationalism has existed in human affairs since time immemorial. Let's cast our net far back in history to see how this was true.

References

Adachi, Nobuko, guest editor, 2010. *East Asian Transnational Migrants and Culture in a Global World. Encounters*, fall.

Biedermann, Reinhard, 2017. "Taiwan's Polycentric Strategy Within the Environmental Regime Complex on Climate Change." *ASIEN*, 143, April: S. 25–46. Located at http://asienforschung.de/wp-content/uploads/2018/03/143_RA_Biedermann_ClimateChange_final.pdf.

Bourne, Randolph S., 1916. "Trans-National America, *The Atlantic*. Accessed 9 March 2022 at https://www.theatlantic.com/magazine/archive/1916/07/trans-national-america/304838/.

Britanica. "Transnationalism." Accessed 12 March 2022 at https://www.britannica.com/topic/transnationalism.

Chen Yu-fu, Kayleigh Madjar, 2022. "Taiwan's Influence Growing, Despite China, Minister Says." *Taipei Times*, 3 May.

Djelic, Marie-Laure, Kerstin Sahlin-Andersson, eds., 2006. *Transnational Governance: Institutional Dynamics of Regulation*. Cambridge UP.

Hau, Caroline S., Kasian Tejapira, 2011. *Traveling Nation-Makers: Transnational Flows and Movement in the Making of Modern Southeast Asia*. NUS Press, in association with Kyoto UP.

Heylen, Ann, 2010. "The Transnational in Taiwan History: A Preliminary Exploration." *Concentric: Literary and Cultural Studies*, 36.1, March 2010: 9–33. Located at http://www.concentric-literature.url.tw/issues/Transnational%20Taiwan/2.pdf.

Huang, S., 2009. "Transnationality: The Logics of Transnationality." In International Encyclopedia of Human Geography. Located at ScienceDirect, "Transnationalism." Accessed 10 March 2022 at https://www.sciencedirect.com/topics/social-sciences/transnationalism.

Kissinger, Henry, 2014. *World Order: Reflections on the Character of Nations and the Course of History*. Penguin Books.

Pendery, David, 2022. "Taiwan Diplomacy: Worth the Effort?" *Taiwan Insight*. Taiwan Studies Programme at the University of Nottingham. 8 March. Located at https://taiwaninsight.org/2022/03/07/taiwan-diplomacy-worth-the-effort/.

Robinson, William I., 1998. "Beyond Nation-State Paradigms: Globalization, Sociology, and the Challenge of Transnational Studies." *Sociological Forum*, 13.4.

Sørensen, Ninna Nyberg, 2007. *Living Across Worlds: Diaspora, Development and Transnational Engagement*. International Organization for Migration.

Thoughtco. "What Is Transnationalism? Definition, Pros, and Cons." Located at https://www.thoughtco.com/what-is-transnationalism-definition-pros-and-cons-5073163.

Wikipedia. "Cultural Trait." Located at https://en.wikipedia.org/wiki/Cultural_trait.

———. "Transnationalism." Located at https://en.wikipedia.org/wiki/Transnationalism.

Yeoh, Brenda S.A., Katie Willis, 2004. *State/Nation/Transnation: Perspectives on Transnationalism in the Asia-Pacific*. Routledge.

CHAPTER 2

Out of Taiwan: A Transnational Take

Abstract This chapter includes an examination of the "Out of Taiwan" thesis as the possibility that the origins and settlement of nations and empires in the Austronesian region may stem from the migration of peoples out of Taiwan, possibly as far back as the Neolithic age. There is first mention of Taiwan indigenous peoples, and their relation to this. Introduction of Taiwanese aboriginal Asan Surot, and his ideas and views on Out of Taiwan and its impact in his tribe. Look at recent Taiwanese immigration and diaspora as a new look at Out of Taiwan, and relation to the Chinese diaspora. Examination of Taiwanese students and others as core to the new diaspora. First look at migration and diaspora in terms of transnationalism, and Taiwan's continued travels mirroring Out of Taiwan.

Keywords Out of Taiwan · Austronesian/Indo-Pacific region. Taiwan diaspora · Chinese diaspora · Asan Surot · Taiwan indigenous peoples · New Taiwan diaspora · Taiwanese students

"Out of Taiwan" refers to the possibility that the origins and settlement of nations and empires in the Austronesian/Indo-Pacific region, as well as languages across the Indo-Pacific region, may stem from the migration of peoples out of Taiwan, possibly as far back as the Neolithic age (see

D. Pendery, *Transnational Taiwan*,
https://doi.org/10.1007/978-981-19-4368-3_2

Kuo). This theory was originated by linguist Robert Blust (1940–2022) and later voiced from an archaeological perspective by professor Peter Bellwood (emeritus professor of archaeology at the School of Archaeology and Anthropology of the Australian National University).

Simply put, "The very geographical position of Taiwan Island puts it at the crossroads of maritime, cross-cultural, and interactional connections in the wake of the age of discovery" (Heylen 9). Ko et al. write "analysis allows us to reconstruct a history of early Austronesians arriving in Taiwan in the north—6,000 years ago, spreading rapidly to the south, and leaving Taiwan—4,000 years ago to spread throughout Island Southeast Asia, Madagascar, and Oceania," and "The expansion of the Austronesian language family, one of the world's largest expansions across Island Southeast Asia and Oceania, began in Taiwan" (no page number). Recently, the *Taipei Times* reported that a "treasure trove" of prehistoric shell tools had been found in Taiwan, which suggested contact and relations between far-flung Indo-Pacific communities. "The burial site on Oluanpi (鵝鑾鼻), Taiwan's southernmost tip," reported the newspaper, "contains a trove of artifacts dating back 3,800 to 4,200 years," which was stated by National Tsing Hua University associate professor of anthropology Chiu Hung-lin (邱鴻霖), who is leading the expedition along with anthropology professor Li Kuang-ti (李匡悌)." The finding "proves early interaction between the peoples in Taiwan and overseas, having significant implications for Austronesian studies," said Chiu. We see therefore further evidence of what the Out of Taiwan thesis may indicate. The Out of Taiwan model "[is] largely supported by archeological data and the linguistic phylogeny of Austronesian languages" (Jinam 33), and in a word, "DNA and language show that there is a connection between the indigenous people of Taiwan and the people of the Pacific" (National Geographic TW). The Taiwan Council of Indigenous Peoples in turn reports that Taiwan has long been inhabited by Austronesian Linguistic families. The range of this spread of peoples and language extends from Madagascar in Southeast Africa across the Indian Ocean to Easter Island in the Pacific Ocean and from Taiwan in the north to New Zealand in the south. Taiwan is the northernmost region where the Austronesian linguistic family is found, and travel from northern origins to south is probably most likely. The Austronesian speakers living in Taiwan are found in various tribes, including mountains and plains groups. Though research has found this linguistic link, many of the Taiwan indigenous peoples have lost their original language, and revitalization efforts are under way.

I am told that although no indigenous peoples in Taiwan actually recognize Out of Taiwan with a ritual or festival celebration, the government actively promotes and extends the idea worldwide.

Kuo goes on that "Taiwan was a link between continental East Asia and the Pacific, and [is] an important [cultural and geographical] stepping stone that facilitated interaction between Asia–Pacific prehistoric maritime cultures" (1, 3), and that the "geographical and cultural complexity" of Taiwan's indigenous peoples "can…be attributed to Taiwan's special position in the Asia–Pacific maritime culture and its contacts with external cultures" (3). Indeed, we might view here that Taiwan's "Oceanic, transnational perspective…is driven by a desire on the part of local, marginalized peoples to break out of historiographical marginality and isolation" (Heylen 23), conceptions that will be seen again in the following.

Common heritage has been observed linking Taiwan with most other Indo-Pacific islands in terms of cultural artifacts and characteristics, including tattooing (facial tattooing is commonly found in Taiwanese Atayal indigenous peoples), use of outriggers on canoes (all Austronesian peoples out of Taiwan used and continued to use these craft; these "were the vessels that enabled the Austronesian expansion from Taiwan into the islands of both the Indian and Pacific Ocean" [Wikipedia, "Outrigger boat"]), features of ethnographic and prehistoric art styles, and social characteristics such as concern with birth order of siblings (seen in the Amis, Paiwan, and other Taiwan tribes), and a reverence for ancestral kin group founders (found often in Taiwanese indigenous celebrations, which we will examine further, below).

Interestingly enough, Asan Surot, a native Amis Taiwan indigenous person (a native language translator with an American father), tells me that a myth/legend in his people actually looks at their migration in reverse, that is to say they have tales telling the stories of how they ***arrived in Taiwan***, generally by way of island-hopping that brought them here. From here, their native tales go on to explain how the Amis, the largest indigenous tribe in Taiwan, spread all across the island, with pockets of them now found from north to south and east to west. He adds that nowadays, any idea of "migration" almost exclusively concerns the movement of the Amis people from their villages into urban areas in Taiwan—a common story with most Taiwan indigenous peoples. Surot tells me that the Amis people have the words for "right" and "left," but they rarely use them, and instead they use a "hemispheric" system to identify locations, using, roughly, north, south, east, and west. This might well point to a traveling culture (the same is in part true in the Mandarin language).

Further evidence has shown that "Pacific populations originated in Taiwan around 5,200 years ago," and migration from Taiwan "played a major role in the spread of people throughout the world" (*Science Daily*). This possible source of Austronesian peoples and their great civilizations is compelling, and is probably at least in part true (although the possibility that Austronesia was founded by peoples from China or other Asian nations are also likelihoods).

Blust has said, "the Austronesian expansion out of Taiwan, which reached more than halfway around the globe, is one of the great chapters in human history. The phenomenon deserves a place in historical accounts" (from *Taiwan Today*). I would add that it deserves a place in *transnational* historical accounts! Although Taiwanese peoples are not traveling in these modes or using these methods today, they are still very much traveling "out" into the world—and we will see much more of this in our look at modern-day diasporas below. And this is to say nothing of all of the foreigners traveling *in* to Taiwan, yielding a booming, flourishing, altogether pioneering and innovative populations of many, many nationalities making their homes in Taiwan, and in immeasurable ways collaborating and connecting with the locals. It is just this back-and-forth, this pillar of trans- and interactivity of peoples of all types that is the very essence of transnational communities in the world today—and perhaps nowhere do we see this more in play than in Taiwan. The transnational time is now in Taiwan, and virtually every foreigner, and the majority of Taiwanese who live here, are thinking exactly this.

Now, let's continue back into history in the following, "The Silk Road: The First Appearance of Transnationalism?".

References

Heylen, Ann 2010. "The Transnational in Taiwan History: A Preliminary Exploration." *Concentric: Literary and Cultural Studies*, 36.1, March 2010: 9–33. Located at http://www.concentric-literature.url.tw/issues/Transnational%20Taiwan/2.pdf.

Hung Mei-hsiu, Kayleigh Madjar, with staff writer and CNA, 28 July 2022. *Taipei Times*, "Treasure trove of prehistoric tools found in Oluanpi."

Locatedd at https://www.taipeitimes.com/News/taiwan/archives/2022/07/28/2003782567.

Jinam, Timothy adrian Anak Joseph, 2011. "The Genetic diversity and population history of indigenous peoples in Asia" Dissertation, Department of Genetics, School of Life Science, The Graduate University for Advanced Studies (SOKENDAI). Accessed 5 February, 2022 at https://ir.soken.ac.jp/index.php?active_action=repository_view_main_item_detail&page_id=29&block_id=155&item_id=2706&item_no=1.

Ko, Albert Min-Shan, Chung-Yu Chen, Qiaomei Fu, Frederick Delfin, Mingkun Li, Hung-Lin Chiu, Mark Stoneking, Ying-Chin Ko, 2014. "Early Austronesians: Into and Out of Taiwan." Am J Hum Genet. 2014 Mar 6; 94(3): 426–436. Accessed 10 March, 2022 at https://www.ncbi.nlm.nih.gov/pmc/articles/PMC3951936/.

Kuo, Su-chiu, 2019. "New Frontiers in the Neolithic Archaeology of Taiwan (5600–1800 BP): A Perspective of Maritime Cultural Interaction." *The Archaeology of Asia-Pacific Navigation*, Volume 3, Springer, Chunming Wu, Series Editor. Accessed 7 January, 2022 at https://www.academia.edu/43631953/New_Frontiers_in_the_Neolithic_Archaeology_of_Taiwan_5600_1800_BP_A_Perspective_of_Maritime_Cultural_Interaction

National Geographic TW. "Secrets of the Ocean Tribes." Accessed 7 January, 2022 at https://www.youtube.com/watch?v=bC1H-UI57hE.

Pendery, David, 2020. *Taiwan—A Light in the East: A Personal and Analytical Taiwan Study*, Palgrave Macmillan.

———, 2018. "Taiwanese settling far and wide: a global view," *Taipei Times*, 5 February. 2018. Located at https://www.taipeitimes.com/News/editorials/archives/2018/02/05/2003687071

Said, Edward W., 1993–1994. *Culture and Imperialism*. Vintage Books.

Science Daily, 27 January, 2009. "Pacific people spread from Taiwan, language evolution, study shows." Source, U of Auckland. Accessed 2 February, 2022 at https://www.sciencedaily.com/releases/2009/01/090122141146.htm.

Statista. "Number of students from Taiwan studying abroad in academic year 2019/20, by major destination countries." Located at https://www.statista.com/statistics/1092368/taiwan-students-studying-abroad-by-destination-country/.

Surot, Asan, 28 March, 2022. Personal interview, Taipei, Taiwan.

Taiwan Today, 2021. "CIP launches book on origins of the Austronesians." Accessed 28 March, 2022 at https://nspp.mofa.gov.tw/nsppe/print.php?post=206280&unit=381.

Wikipedia, "Outrigger boat." Located at https://en.wikipedia.org/wiki/Outrigger.

CHAPTER 3

The Silk Road: The First Appearance of Transnationalism?

Abstract This chapter provides an introduction of the Silk Road as the first historical appearance of transnationalism. Continued examination of the historical aspects of the Silk Road, with deliveries of goods and products across borders in Asia, Africa and Europe, emergence of transnational merchant classes, and the rise and fall of empires. Mention of major Silk Road travelers of the past. Examination of the Silk Road's vital role in opening political and economic relations between nations, with associated technological, cultural, educational and social advances. As travelers encountered new cultures, they brought developments back to their homelands, opening new areas of learning and international understanding, and artistic and aesthetic influences. The decline of the Silk Road is examined, and the modern introduction of new Silk Road developments and.initiatives through China, the European Bank for Reconstruction and Development, and others, with a nod toward including Taiwan more completely in the present day.

Keywords Silk Road · International routes · Goods · Commodities · Religion · Aesthetics · Arts · Cultural advances · China · EBRD · Taiwan

D. Pendery, *Transnational Taiwan*,
https://doi.org/10.1007/978-981-19-4368-3_3

I include a question mark in the above title, because the truth is that we could no doubt go back further into history to explore the emergence and development of the transnational concept. But let's start here. The Silk Road, of course, was the network of Eurasian trade routes active from the second century BC until the mid-fifteenth century, spanning thousands of miles from east to west, north to south. Linking China and other Asian nations with India, Europe, Africa, and Arab countries, the routes played a central role in facilitating economic, cultural, political, and religious interactions between all the countries, from ancient times to the middle ages. Needless to say, the importance of the Silk Road in history and human relations cannot be overestimated. Chinese silk and porcelains were initially sought in Rome, Egypt, and Greece, but many other regions and nations soon followed suit. Other commodities shipped from the East included teas, dyes, and perfumes, while Western nations and others exported horses, camels, honey, wine, and gold back to China and other nations. To be sure, we see here an early instance of international transnationalism, and a reduction of the importance of boundaries. In addition to generating considerable wealth for the emergent merchant classes (who themselves became and would continue to be principal transnational groups), the proliferation and sharing of goods—including horses introduced to China contributing to the might of the Mongol Empire, paper and gunpowder *from* China that helped spread literature and literacy, and changed the very nature of war in Europe and beyond—altered the course of world history (*National Geographic Society, World History Encyclopedia*).

During its roughly 1,500 years of existence, the Silk Road endured the rise and fall of numerous empires and experienced several major catastrophes. A highly decentralized network, security was not strong, and travelers consistently faced threats by thieves, brigands, and raiders. That did not stop major travelers like Marco Polo (Venetian), William of Rubruck (Flemish), Benedykt Polak (Polish), Giovanni da Pian del Carpine (Italian), and Andrew of Longjumeau (Dominican). These adventurers saw the Silk Road as a succession of middlemen, brokers, jobbers, go-betweens, and distributors, which peppered the entire passage, and facilitated the incredible exchange of goods, ideas and peoples.

As noted, the Silk Road trade played a vital role in opening political and economic relations between nations. "We think of globalisation as a uniquely modern phenomenon; yet 2,000 years ago, it was a fact of life, one that presented opportunities, created problems and prompted technological advance," writes Peter Frankopan (professor of global history at Oxford University; from Clark). As well as varieties of products, the road facilitated an unrivaled exchange of languages, ideas, education, religions, philosophies, viewpoints and scientific discoveries, virtually all of which were incorporated into the various societies along the way. Religion and ideas spread along the Silk Road in a flood of very much transnational influence, and Zoroastrianism, Judaism, Buddhism, Christianity, Manichaeism, and Islamism all extended widely across Eurasia and Asia (and not a little in Europe and elsewhere) through the routes. Migrants, refugees, exiles, missionaries, artisans, diplomats, and soldiers traveled widely, opening these first true instances of transnationality. Such intellectual and cultural exchanges yielded new centers of culture and learning. Cities along the route developed as multicultural metropolises, teeming with interactions of all kinds. As travelers absorbed the cultures they encountered, they brought them back to their homelands, opening new vistas of learning and international understanding.

Many artistic and aesthetic influences were conveyed and communicated via the Silk Road, with Asian, European, Hellenistic, Iranian, and Indian inspirations mingling. The mobility among peoples traveling the many paths, by land and sea, introduced into varied cultures new arts, philosophies, and concepts, and played a key role in enabling intercultural contacts and exchanges. These overall exchanges of information, politics, fine arts, religious conceptions, technologies, and simple human interactivity gave rise to innovations that changed the world, as we have seen. Today, many areas on the Silk Road are listed as UNESCO World Heritage sites, further indicating their universal importance and impact.

After surviving many geopolitical changes and disruptions, the Silk Road ended with the rise of the Ottoman Empire, which severed most trade between the East and the West. This prompted efforts to seek alternate avenues to Eastern products, thereby ushering in European colonialism and imperialism, and in essence a wider process of transnational globalization (more on this below). The network's influence survives into the twenty-first century, however, and a restart is now seen in China's Belt and Road Initiative (BRI), which aims to construct transportation and infrastructure projects across the different regions, and increase trade between the East and the West. China has signed BRI agreements with upwards of 138 countries, running into the billions of dollars, and the future looks to be a route connecting China across Asia to Europe and

Africa. Chinese President Xi Jinping has said that the BRI will provide a wealth of opportunities and positive outcomes that will benefit the world, and that China "has no geopolitical motives, seeks no exclusionary blocs, and imposes no business deals on others" (*Xinhuanet*). Not a few people have disagreed here, and see this move as a likely predatory move by China that will result in huge debt problems in countries that seek infrastructure improvement and trade opportunities. I will not examine this criticism here.

Admittedly, I am not aware of any actual mention of Taiwan in the Silk Road historical accounts, and the island's actual location appears to put it outside of the actual trade routes. But we might view the close connection of Taiwan and China business and commercial interests, and see them as essentially one of a common fabric, and we can connect Taiwan, broadly to these experiences, in this way. And today, there is more. The Taiwan ports of Kaohsiung and Taipei have been included as container shipping services embraced by the Silk Road Maritime International Forum, an action launched in December 2018 by Fujian Provincial Communication Transportation Group, China Cosco Shipping Corp, and Xiamen Port Group, in order to offer a shipping platform under China's Belt and Road Initiative (from *The LoadStar)*. It is also now said that the European Bank for Reconstruction and Development (EBRD) is investing in a "New Silk Road" that retraces the Silk Road of ancient times (in cooperation with the Chinese Belt and Road imitative). Beginning in the Xinjiang Chinese autonomous region (新疆维吾尔自治区), the new initiative passes through Kazakhstan, and winds its way through Moscow on the way to its final destination in St. Petersburg, Russia. Completion of the New Silk Road is expected to cut travel time between Zhengzhou City (郑州市) in Henan Province (河南省) and St. Petersburg from 45 to 14 days. It is felt that the New Silk Road could open up Central Asian markets for Taiwan (from *Taiwan Panorama*). "Stretching from Central Asia to Central and Eastern Europe to Northern Africa, the EBRD's areas of operation cover many strategic nodes along the One Belt One Road initiative," said Wang Yanzhi, board member and president of the Silk Road Fund (from *GTR)*. We see here and above that the Silk Road does not appear to have "ended" after all, and that it is taking on new shapes in the twenty-first century—with Taiwan included this time.

Following is a bit more historical analysis and overview, "Colonialism, Imperialism: The Next Phase of Transnationalism," areas in which we will very much see Taiwan accounts and peoples.

References

Clark, Greg, 2016. "How cities took over the world: A history of globalisation spanning 4,000 years." *The Guardian*. Located at https://www.theguardian.com/cities/2016/dec/01/how-cities-took-over-the-world-a-history-of-globalisation-spanning-4000-years.

Global Trade Review (GTR), "EBRD to work together with Silk Road Fund" Located at https://www.gtreview.com/news/asia/ebrd-to-work-together-with-silk-road-fund/.

Goodreads. Located at https://www.goodreads.com/.

The LoadStar, "Taiwan ports of Kaohsiung and Taipei embraced by Silk Road shipping platform," Located at https://theloadstar.com/taiwan-ports-of-kaohsiung-and-taipei-embraced-by-silk-road-shipping-platform/.

Taiwan Panorama, "The New Silk Road," Located at https://www.taiwan-panorama.com/en/Articles/Details?Guid=06fca070-7058-4840-bc67-98f39c267c84&CatId=9&postname=The%20New%20Silk%20Road.

National Geographic Society, "The Silk Road," accessed 3 March, 2022 at https://www.nationalgeographic.org/encyclopedia/silk-road/.

Xinhuanet. "Xi Focus-Quotable Quotes: Xi Jinping on Belt and Road Initiative." Accessed 5 March, 2022 at http://www.xinhuanet.com/english/2020-09/07/c_139349475.htm.

Wikipedia. "Silk Road." Located at https://en.wikipedia.org/wiki/Silk_Road.

World History Encyclopedia, "Paper in Ancient China." Located at https://www.worldhistory.org/article/1120/paper-in-ancient-china/.

CHAPTER 4

Colonialism, Imperialism: The Next Phase of Transnationalism

Abstract This chapter includes an examination of global colonialism and imperialism, their impact worldwide and in Taiwan, with a look at how transnational aspects are included in these actions. It includes a look at how "metropolitan" centers of power created these developments worldwide. Edward W. Said is introduced as a principal writer on imperialism. There is a look at "subjects" and "others" in the colonial and imperial worlds, and an "us versus them" mentality. Positive results created by colonialism and imperialism are looked at, as well as negative effects. Consideration of slavery as an instance of transnational relocation of peoples in America. English colonization of the U.S. and Japanese colonization of Taiwan, with positive and negative effects are looked at. Dutch and Spanish colonization of Taiwan, and the arrival of the Kuomintang party in Taiwan after the Chinese Civil War.

Keywords Transnationalism · Colonialism · Imperialism · Taiwan · Colonization—Japanese · Dutch · Spanish · English · Us versus them · The other · Subjects · Metropolitan powers · Edward W. Said

To move ahead, let's consider the abovementioned ages of colonialism and imperialism, from about 1500 to the early twentieth century (by which time the age of transnational globalization was pretty much fully

D. Pendery, *Transnational Taiwan*,
https://doi.org/10.1007/978-981-19-4368-3_4

apparent), and in some senses beyond, into the late twentieth century (when any idea of imperialism as centered on the United States). Before we consider these ideas, let's take a look at a time and place a bit earlier than this, where we can see a transnational take in the migratory movements and exchanges among a small group of people in a much smaller part of the world, in the south of France and north of Spain. Here I refer to the work of historian Emmanuel Le Roy Ladurie (born 1929), who in his great work *Montaillou*, drew a picture of the people in a small French village, Montaillou, and neighboring provinces and parishes, which provides a fascinating look at what can be seen as an early instance of transnational exchanges of languages, values, and lifestyles—if in a much smaller scope and range than we are generally considering here. Ladurie sees a "great migration" that took place among these peoples (shepherds and other animal workers, small-scale artisans, food makers, and groups of more elite people such as priests, bailiffs, and other governors) as they moved back and forth among the localities in this region, viewing these movements and exchanges as an "exodus," "diaspora," and simply groups of mobile refugees (Ladurie 89 and passim). In words that echo my own, he portrays "the flood of migrants, shepherds, unemployed and misfits" that make up a "human transhumance" across the borders of France and Spain (89; the transhumance is a seasonal movement of livestock between fixed summer and winter pastures, and has been called "a type of…nomadism" by Wikipedia). All of these "ideological migrations" (98) comprised a "long march" (102) made up of "networks of patronage, friendship, complicity and compaternity" (92) which engaged the peoples in complex ways, both hostile and affable. These peoples generally formed themselves into close-knit families, homesteads, and social units, which would then be extended out across the local and more-distant areas, creating the linked local-distant connections I will refer to. These "great movements of migration" (111) created "cultural cross-roads" (109), first centered on the home, but stretching out into "totally different geographical origin[s] and identity" (109), yielding "transhistorical trends" (110), and new "social position[s] and mental outlook[s]" (120). During all of this, the people's "destiny was a destination" (135), and "the people on both sides of the frontier all really belonged to the same world" (239), mirroring all we have seen and will see in the forthcoming. Ladurie gives us an early look, a microcosm of the greater trends we will see springing forth in the coming centuries.

Colonialism the policies and practices of acquiring political control over another country, and then occupying it and exploiting it economically—and imperialism—the policies and practices of extending "metropolitan" (from Said) power and dominion over distant regions by way of territorial acquisitions and seizing control over the political and economic life, usually accompanied with "a sense of mission, historical necessity, and evangelical fervor" (Richard J. Barnet cited in Said 286), extended the reach of peoples and countries across countless borders. Such practices were by no means always positive or appealing to the "subjects" and "others" who were controlled. An exhaustive "us versus them" culture emerged from colonialism/imperialism, giving rise to an "almost metaphysical obligation to rule subordinate, inferior or less advanced peoples" (Said 10, and more on this culture below). This was very much a world of "barbarities, tyrannies and degradations" (Said 21), facilitated by an essentialist description of "others" that "absolves and forgives ignorance and demagogy more than it enables knowledge" (Said 31, reworded), made up of "marginalized and/or subjugated subjects confined to secondary spots in the curricula in metropolitan centers" (Said 316). In a word, and to continue, these practices "reveal a remarkable arrogance," wherein colonial/imperial European powers "redrew the borders of ancient nations, oblivious that this might be an abnormal, unwelcome or illegitimate development" (Kissinger 173–174).

In spite of the above, colonialism and imperialism yielded positive results, in some respects. Edward W. Said, to be sure a principal researcher in imperialism, has said that after a "general world-wide pattern of [always dominating, always abusive, always cumulative] imperial culture" (xii, reworded) from the 1800s into the twentieth century, a "historical experience of resistance against empire" (xii) arose, leading to liberation movements, decolonization, and the composition of "grand narratives of emancipation and enlightenment," (xiii) which "mobilized people in the colonial world to rise up and throw off imperial subjection," (xiii) leading to "the end of empire" (my quotes). The result was "an impressive roster of newly empowered voices asking for their narratives to be heard" (xx), and "the creation of associations and parties whose common goal was self-determination and national independence" (xii). Ultimately, "One of imperialism's achievements was to bring the world closer together" (a "fully global world" Said also says) (xxi, 6). And yet more, "Partly because of empire, all cultures are involved in one another, none is single and pure, all are hybrid, heterogeneous, extraordinarily differentiated, and unmonolithic" (xxv). This all begins to sound like transnational endeavor.

Imperialism and colonialism, perhaps in Said's sense, introduced new languages, and essential diplomatic, societal, economic, and political practices across borders and regions. As well, "colonial states led to migration for the purposes of administration, labour recruitment and trade" (Yeoh 17), further widening the transnational experience and impact.

While such colonialism brings many negative effects, it does represent a certain "transnational" meeting of cultures, and there are some benefits that emerge from this. Said says that colonialism/imperialism introduced a "vaster reality" linking homelands and newlands, made up of a group that in some senses mirrors my own above, with "scholars, administrators, travelers, traders, theorists, parliamentarians, merchants, novelists, speculators, adventurers, visionaries, poets, and every variety of outcast and misfit" contributing to life in the varying outlying possessions (9).

Such "invaders" can:

1. Bring new cultural patterns into a newland (often very much for the worse, but sometimes for the better)
2. Expand educational opportunity
3. Enlarge economic ties
4. Introduce new languages (also for better and worse)
5. Spur modernization, technological advancement, and the discovery of new resources
6. In some senses, encourage the native peoples to band together more tightly, introducing new regional placements, a given mobility, the rise of cities, the actual rejection of colonial masters, and the like.

We saw all of this, for example, in the English colonization of what would become the United States—the formation of which brought about some of the most innovative and significant political and social changes in history, reverberating across nations worldwide. As well, the English colonization of India, though troubled in many serious ways and giving rise to much violence and discriminatory behavior, itself resulted in the emergence of one of the most important democracies in the present day. Kissinger himself notes this, and in India "Western intrusion…reshaped a great civilization into a modern state" (192), and inspired India "to constitute itself as a [free, democratic] nation" (200, with added text).

As well, in a transnational turn, "India has long developed its qualities at the intersection of world orders, shaping and being shaped by their rhythms. It has been defined less by its political borders than by a shared spectrum of cultural traditions" (192; Taiwan, we might add, is quite similar, and we will see this in the forthcoming text). China, he notes, is similar, and has "imposed its own matrix of customs and culture on invaders so successfully that they grew indistinguishable from the Chinese people" (192–193).

In these lights, the insertion of new languages into newlands, though problematic ("language shift," the process by which members of a native community abandon their original vernacular or language in favor of another imported arrival, is one problem), does have importance in this transnational view.

We might also say that the introduction of the English language into India initiated new linguistic narratives and views onto life that have had very positive and valuable results (and as well has initiated technological and scientific innovation into Indian society in vital ways). Such introduction of non-native languages became common in Taiwan during various colonial eras, up until Japanese rule, and for that matter, after. This has been an overall positive, and the study of foreign languages continues to be very popular in Taiwan today. The nation's aim is to be a bilingual (Chinese and English) society by as early as 2030. The aim is for the country to develop bilingual skills in the following areas and operations (from Financial Supervisory Commission):

- The educational system
- English media
- Tourism
- Public–private partnerships
- Legal services
- English proficiency across all major industries
- Youth and cultural activities
- The use of English in civil exercises.[1]

[1] We might note here that one criticism of this plan is that it "ignores the other languages in Taiwan that make millions of Taiwanese already bilingual or multi-lingual, and overlooks Taiwan's multiethnic population," as said by Taiwan Languages and Literature Society director Chiang Min-hua (江敏華). "English plans 'ignore' linguistic diversity" Jason Pan, *Taipei Times*, 9 April 2022.

In all of this, we see true transnational qualities.

Taiwan has most certainly experienced ages of imperialism and colonialism, principally by way of the arrival of Dutch colonialists in the island in the 1600 s, followed by the arrival of the Spanish at the same time, and from there the influence of China by the 1800s and, perhaps most importantly, during the colonial domination of Japan (1895–1945). Along the way came the influence and arrival of a number of other Western nations (See my *Taiwan: A Light in the East* for a more extended look at the colonial eras in Taiwan). For the most part, all of the advantages (and all of the disadvantages) noted above were brought to Taiwan by the Dutch, Spanish, Chinese, and Japanese colonialists(And see below, "Transnational Experience: Indigenous Peoples, Reprise" for a further look at colonialism in Taiwan, in particular its impact on these indigenous peoples). Interestingly, the Japanese colonization and associated imperialism in Taiwan, while negative in many respects, yielded much positive in the nation, not least the development of the train system (vital in Taiwanese life to this day), the extension of education, urban planning, and very significant scientific research and discoveries. I have before said that Japan and Taiwan, troubled history though they experienced, are in fact "sister nations" in the present day that very much like each other.[2]

I will not comment here on to what extent the arrival of the ruling Kuomintang party after its defeat in the Civil War in China gave rise to an autocratic "colonial" rule in Taiwan. I may be stretching the point in all we have looked at to call colonialism and imperialism "transnationalism," but I think a valid point has been made.

[2] As an aside, in terms of the above, I have never given thought to the idea of slavery in the United States and other countries, broadly, in these respects, and the way slaves were transported from their homelands into newlands, and what this might imply. Few would think of slaves as "transnationals" in the true sense—voluntary activity that it is always supposed to be. Nevertheless, the blossoming of black/African American culture post-slavery in the United States to be sure deeply changed and influenced (white) American culture, and this could be seen as an epic transnational awakening (and the same could be said about almost any other country that had slavery). This could be a further study of its own—how exactly slaves were, in effect, "transnationals" in new homes, inducing new cultural experience and values, learning new languages, etc. I will not pursue this thought here.

References

Financial Supervisory Commission, Republic of China. "Taiwan's 2030 goal to become a bilingual nation." Located at https://www.fsc.gov.tw/en/home.jsp?id=253&parentpath=0,4,212,252.

Kissinger, Henry, 2014. *World Order: Reflections on the Character of Nations and the Course of History*. Penguin Books.

Ladurie, Emmanuel Le Roy, 1978. *Montaillou*. Penguin Books.

Pan, Jason, *Taipei Times*, 9 April 2022. "English plans 'ignore' linguistic diversity."

Said, Edward W., 1993–1994. *Culture and Imperialism*. Vintage Books.

Yeoh, Brenda S.A., Katie Willis. 2004. *State/Nation/Transnation: Perspectives on Transnationalism in the Asia-Pacific*. Routledge.

CHAPTER 5

Out of SE Asia: A New Transnational Network

Abstract This chapter includes a look at the new SE Asian diaspora, and how Asian transnational migration is taking on importance around the world. There is a continued examination of the new Taiwan diaspora, and its relation to the Chinese diaspora is examined. Examined is the opening of transnational business ventures worldwide, and engagement of transnational migrants in politics abroad and in their homelands. The SE Asian transnational network as a "transplanted global society," with exchanges of ideas, products, ideologies, world views, and cultural artifacts is examined. Assimilation in new countries post WWII and Cold War, as well as exclusion of new migrants in "newlands." First introduction of multiculturalism in these respects. Taiwan as central to the SE Asian diaspora, and introduction of transnational business and work. Chinese migration to the UK, and Japanese transnational subjects in Brazil are examined, as well as retained homeland connections of Japanese in Brazil. Extended looks at stories of Taiwanese transnationals Judy Chen and Ciloue Cheng Stewart.

Keywords SE Asian diaspora · Chinese diaspora · Taiwanese diaspora · Transnational network · Cultural artifacts · WWII Cold War · Multiculturism · Brazil · UK · Judy Chen · Ciloue Cheng Stewart

D. Pendery, *Transnational Taiwan*,
https://doi.org/10.1007/978-981-19-4368-3_5

A new diaspora emerging out of SE Asia has emerged in recent years, and is now taking on importance around the world. Adachi writes that "East Asians are one of the fastest growing transnational migrant populations in the world today" (9). Simply put, "Asian and Pacific countries have a long history of permanent or cyclical migration for purposes of trade, work, religion, or cultural exchange" (Yeoh 17). In a word, SE Asia has "experienced a marked increase in the size of [its] migrant populations over the past two decades" (UNDESA 9), and "witnessed large increases in their transnational populations"—upwards of 38 million in 2020 (UNDESA 15). These Asian transnational migrants (and, to repeat, immigrants, travelers, tourists, aliens, expatriates, evacuees, exiles, refugees, and nomads)[1] are playing new roles internationally in the cultural, social, political, and economic development of the world—both locally and internationally, in both newlands and homelands (we see this conception again and will see it often going forward).[2]

We might view Taiwan as "East Asia," but I think we can fairly take the island nation into this view of migrancy and transnational travels—and we have already seen pointed evidence of just this. We have viewed Taiwan's more ancient take on that which is transnational (Out of Taiwan), and we will continue to see more figures in the following on just how many Taiwanese people are traveling across borders in the present day. Thinking back to the great ancient exodus of the Out of Taiwan peoples, and the origins it gave rise to, will no doubt cast light on Taiwan's rich past and help to solidify and amalgamate Taiwanese identity, but I think a look at the modern-day Taiwan diaspora might be even more compelling and relevant.

The Taiwanese diaspora, proper, began in the early twentieth century, perhaps principally after the conclusion of the first Sino-Japanese War. After the Treaty of Shimonoseki, awarding Taiwan sovereignty to Japan, it was agreed that the inhabitants of Taiwan would be permitted to sell their property and leave the island. A small percentage of the population chose

[1] And we should note here that Southeast Asia produced 2.1 million forced migrants in 2021, almost 300,000 who were refugees and asylum-seekers (from Chen).

[2] We should note here that Europe was the region with the largest number of international migrants in 2020 at 87 million. North America had almost 59 million, followed by North Africa and West Asia, with a total of nearly 50 million. If trends continue, North Africa and West Asia will overtake North America as the region with the second largest number of migrants in the world within the next few decades (from UNDESA).

to return to China, and an unknown number fled as refugees to other countries in the Indo-Pacific Region, and to some Western countries. After this time, by the 1950s, the true modern Taiwanese diaspora began, principally to Western countries. It was at this time that many students began to study in the West, which will be looked at again below. As well, Taiwanese moved to different countries to buy homes, experience new cultures, open businesses, start families, and raise children in bicultural settings. In the big current picture, the majority of overseas Taiwanese live in the United States, with 1.04 million people of Taiwanese descent living in the country, and Canada, with 69,550–173,000. 404,000 Taiwanese live in China, many of them businesspersons and students (from Directorate-General of Budget, Accounting and Statistics, Executive Yuan, Republic of China, Taiwan; Wikipedia, "Overseas Taiwanese" and "Taiwanese People").

We see that Taiwanese students have in many ways been at the core of this modern migration, as they have traveled to other countries in great numbers for the past 70 years. Taiwanese have studied in the United States since the 1950s, long before Chinese students began to study there in larger numbers. These students and other Taiwanese have been called a "first wave" of immigration to the United States. Taiwan itself in 2019–20 had approximately 24,000 students studying in the United States, and 71,488 students studying in different countries around the world (from *Statista*). It has been said that Taiwanese Americans have the highest educational attainment ranking in the United States, surpassing any other ethnic group or country.

Other Taiwanese have also been migrating to the United States. Upwards of 1.04 million Taiwanese in the country—and many more of Taiwanese descent (from Directorate-General of Budget, Accounting and Statistics, Executive Yuan, Republic of China, Taiwan). This is far fewer than the 5,143,982 Chinese immigrants in the country, but is by no means insignificant (Wikipedia, "Overseas Chinese").

In a word, Taiwan "has a strong diasporic community.... This makes it a window into the world system of territorial sovereignty," says Professor Sanjoy Bannerjee of the Department of International Relations at San Francisco State University.

Taiwanese students, working professionals, scientific personnel, and families have been migrating since the 1950s and before, again reflecting the global perspective of Taiwanese migration. This is truly a global view, with Taiwanese migrating and settling far and wide. (I will look further at Taiwanese transnational education, below.)

This all could be said to be related to the Chinese diaspora, which has been occurring since the mid-1900s and before. The migration of Taiwanese to other lands has been going on for almost as long, but the Taiwan of modern times, by way of which Taiwanese have in a sense found a new identity in their migrations, coheres in important ways with the transnational contemporary world, and these peoples have made a significant impact all around the world.

I am suggesting here that the modern Taiwan diaspora—though it might never match the empires and nations that were given rise to in ancient times—might be no less important to Taiwanese transnational identity and consciousness. In a word, with Taiwan having shaped the modern world in significant ways, giving so much back, their present-day diaspora might one day comprise an epic of its own.

Some have argued that diasporas are precursors to modern transnationalism. The migration of Taiwanese to other countries in modern times has yielded a new Taiwanese transnational identity, a mutual identity, which creates and forges itself across borders and back again. All of this takes place as Taiwan has shaped the modern world in significant ways, and given so much back. It is all comprised of a reciprocity, sharing, collaboration, exchange, and fluidity, a communicative cloverleaf that will take Taiwan into the twenty-first century in the most rewarding and fruitful ways.

I focus on Taiwan here, but more broadly we see an interesting interplay among what might be viewed as the narratives of various identities, whether individual, national, or transnational. All three I think are potentially very strong and influential in people, and should be considered at once separately, and conjointly. The adoption of new languages (to say nothing of new narratives, new histories) in newlands no doubt comes into play in this analysis. Said calls the combination of new conjoint narratives, retellings of one's own and other histories, connections back from newlands to origins, a given pointed (and in some senses resistant, and very much hybrid) "discussion" among varied groups and peoples. He calls it a *voyage in,* a conception I like in terms of our overall analysis, and which seems accurate and pointed in terms of Taiwanese travelers (see Said, 216 and 239).

In a word, all we have discussed "may open up options for transnational participation by Taiwanese [and many other] actors. Taipei's policies comprise national, community, corporate, and societal actors, and aims at securing international support from a variety of sources" (Biedermann 30). The transnational time may be now!

As noted above, we might view the classic Chinese diaspora as the root of all of this development. There are more than 10.7 million Chinese overseas today—about 60 million, if their descendants are included—according to the International Organization for Migration/UN Migration (IOM). Waves of Chinese immigration have resulted in large populations of overseas Chinese in Southeast Asia, North America, Oceania, the Caribbean, South America, Africa, and Europe. This is one of the highest figures of immigration in history. Without question, the Chinese have proven to be a highly "mobile" population, which has "turned them into a truly global diaspora" (Yeoh 17). I will conclude this brief look at the Chinese historical diaspora here.

We might further consider how transnational travelers from Asia have founded transnational businesses (seen in light of actual opening of businesses in newlands, as well as in terms of migrant workers and their employers), engaged in political activity (activism, voting and elections, partisan connections with homelands, solidarity with locals in party/political matters, etc.), created cultural groupings (to some extent to maintain homeland cultural values and connections, but at the same time to adopt the newland ideals), and fashioned social communities (again with communal and communicative connections in homelands and newlands). I may be repeating myself, but these transnational networks, "these systems of ties, interactions, exchanges and mobility," function "intensively…in real time, while being spread throughout the world [that is, in Asia, and everywhere else around the world]" (Yeoh 27, with added text). "Trends towards increased migration, long-term settlement and formation of transnational communities have become inescapable" (Yeoh 27), and in the future, "transnational communities will play an increasingly important role in the Asia–Pacific region" (Yeoh 32)—that is, *within*, but just as assuredly *without*, the region. Perhaps nowhere are these realities truer than for Asian travelers, what is becoming a "transplanted global society" (Adachi 12).

These conceptions comprise "issues that no longer simply exist between migrants and host nations, but also involve aspects of global politics, global economics, international distribution of labor, and global markets" (Adachi 13). The exchanges of ideas, products, ideologies, worldviews, and cultural artifacts may at times be "unruly, chaotic, and unpredictable" (Adachi 13), but they are to be sure fascinating and world-shaking. Castles points out how this Asian diaspora stems from: Political instability (originally after decolonization and new migrations after World War II, followed by the Cold War, but we have certainly seen this in the modern day); and an Asian economic boom and associated travels of businesspersons, entrepreneurs, and migrant workers (to be sure true in Taiwan, and we will return to this below). All we are discussing may result in processes of assimilation in new countries (often preferred by nation-states), by way of which new arrivals learn the local languages, become conversant in local history and geography, and "take on the social and cultural practices of the receiving [nation]" (Yeoh 22). A second approach, less liked by migrants and travelers, is differential exclusion, when host states and peoples refrain from fully welcoming the newcomers, and make efforts to limit their ability to fully ensconce themselves in the new culture (limited housing opportunities, limited freedom to obtain citizenship, a view of them as "temporary sojourners but not long-term residents" [Yeoh 23]). A third possibility is multiculturalism (a melting pot, a nation of hyphenated others, we might say), during which the newcomers are essentially welcomed into the new state and can become permanent citizens—although it remains true that "Transnational communities are groups whose identity is not primarily based on attachment to a specific territory or nation state" (Yeoh 25; Samuel P. Huntington will have much more to say on this, below). This might in fact seem obvious, considering all we have examined about the mobility and flexible attachments of transnationals, and their ongoing attachments to both newlands and homelands. The extent to which Taiwan represents a country of "hyphenated others" in the above terms may be arguable, but to be sure, and as noted, many foreigners from other lands make their home here now (and a number have actually become Taiwanese citizens), and have contributed to all that we have considered. Taiwan has itself been a source of waves of immigrants leaving the nation and region and relocating worldwide, and as much as any other country has become "a contact zone within a larger global context of economic, cultural, and intellectual flows and movements, with travels to, from, and through the region [and any number of other regions] by…" all of the hybrid, plural travelers we have referred to (Hau 2). Upwards of 2.04 million Taiwanese have immigrated overseas in the present day (from Directorate-General of Budget, Accounting and Statistics, Executive Yuan, Republic of China, Taiwan). For more on this, see "Transnational Business and

Work" below. In the following, we will look at the experiences of a few of the travelers we are talking about, from Taiwan, other countries in Asia, and a few other nations, and how the trajectories of these people have resulted in "contingent and uneven processes of translation, circulation, and exchange" (Hau 22).

Chinese migrants to the UK, Pieke, and Biao have found, live within a "mythical landscape of manageable migration that naturalizes the discursive categories that are used to talk about and act on migration" (in Adachi 34). This presents "migration as an external force whose impact upon the receiving society can somehow be managed without migrants themselves having a say in the process" (in Adachi 34). The result of this, the writers say, is a "yawning gap" between fictionalized rhetoric and reality, by way of which, illegal immigrants flow into the UK through the "back door," and many others, "desirable or not" flow through the more-legal "front door" (in Adachi 34), wherein "highly exploitative conditions" result (in Adachi 35). This does not look like a good outcome in our analysis.

Further, Adachi looks at a "commune" in Brazil, Kubo, that was created in 1935, and is populated today by about 100 Japanese migrants. The commune is a farm on which the migrants work, after which they practice various arts in the evening. The Japanese people in the commune "frequently associate with Aliança villagers outside the commune," and in general, though they have found challenges living in this "cashless, arts-oriented" community, have found life in Brazil very pleasing (Adachi 63–65). The commune members have struggled some with their Japanese-ness, as compared to local Brazilians (mixed marriages do occur), and have found that they prefer a given sameness (Japanese-ness, it appears), and "strongly believe that having people who share the same lifestyle or cultural values is more important to Kubo than fresh ideas or new blood" (Adachi 71). Such a tendency toward sameness may be seen in other migrant communities—as I have seen Chinese and Taiwanese travelers in the United States who mostly prefer to be with people who speak their own language, to eat their preferred native cuisines, to associate with familiar homeland histories, etc. (Adachi notes that the Kubo residents do eat both Japanese and Brazilian food.) In the end, these Japanese migrants have in some ways remade themselves as actual Brazilians, but they have also had to "reinvent themselves every day and reshape their identities, their life philosophy, and their ways of living, striving to find a balance between being both Japanese and Brazilian" (Adachi

84). They are striving to "reinforce their…ties with their ancestral nation, Japan, as well as to reinforce their identity as Brazilians at home" (Adachi 85). Sounds very much like many other transnational peoples we have encountered.

Now let's consider some Taiwanese-specific views and stories (and I am inclined to say that these narratives could well be linked to my section "Transnational Subjectivity" below). Taiwanese Judy Chen wrote of transnational travel and coming home in her "Coming Home to a Place I've Never Lived." Schooled in China and the United States, she shares pride and belonging in being educated internationally as a "global citizen," but also finds that she seeks a sense of responsibility, to both her newland and her homeland. In her own belonging and sense of obligation, she struggles with an "anti-nationalistic pride in not knowing any national anthems in full, not belonging to ethnic- or national-identity based student groups in college" (Chen, no page number). Like any other transnational, she seeks understanding of herself, her world, her culture, her community. That's the starting point, she says, "the promise of being part of something, of mastering [one's] environment" (Chen). In this seemingly fractured transnational world, she struggles with "the extent [to] which local, real places seemed abstract," and wrestles with that which is "local," and everything else beyond that (Chen). Her "world," whatever that is exactly given her travels, "seemed exceedingly abstract" and she has "ached for concrete belonging and responsibility" (Chen). She finds comfort in the transnational liminal spaces (and more on these, below), and, "as if standing in the doorway," she notes that what is most important is "being rooted, rooting yourself in place, wherever you are in the world" (Chen). What and where is my place in the world? asks Chen, but she is brought back home and must also ask, What and where is my place in Taiwan? These are the questions that cross every transnational's mind (from Chen, reworded).

Taiwanese Ciloue Cheng Stewart, a Taiwanese student who earned her PhD in the United States, is one person who has experienced all of the above. She has described the transnational network she has encountered in her life in the United States, describing filial-centric networks that comprise "[family] relationships and bonding in which loyalty, commitment and obligations over time [and space] are expected of its members" (1). Stewart here refers to both parents in Taiwan, and to adult Taiwanese students, who are often parents themselves, and who have often graduated and moved into high-level jobs in the United States. These are groups who find their lives are "complicated," "torn between cultural traditions and contemporary challenges," and with "…very different cultural ideologies [not least an 'ideology of family'] and practices" (1, with added text). These families, transnational though they may be, maintain "a fluidity in kinship connections" (2). These relationships "challenge the arbitrary notions" of distinct national boundaries, and can attest to the "interdependent nature of all countries" (2). Stewart found that she questioned her "lived worlds—integrating the co-existent reality of my homeland and my current homebase, my families of origin and procreation, my Chinese-ness and Chinese American-ness" (5; and more on this below). She elucidates here the classic ambiguity felt by transnational persons, wrestling with connections and feelings across home- and newlands. Ultimately, one of her key aims was a search into the filial connections and practices of transnational families, parents, and children, their lived experiences, their new and old connections, their negotiation of "meaning making in the face of changes" (from Stewart 5).

Interestingly enough, for many of these students, the decision to adopt a transnational life overseas was not always clear-cut. It was not necessarily a "long-term vision involving methodical, extensive planning," but instead an "incremental decision," with "one thing leading to another" (Stewart 82). These transnational persons experienced a great deal of ambiguity and doubt about their decisions and processes, and they were not in fact always willing to accept their given American-ness, "even though they all had resident or citizen status" (Stewart 83). They foresaw returning to their homelands, but as often as not were not sure when that day would come. This appears "contrary" to normal expectations of overseas life and adopted transnationality, which has long emerged out of a sense of "adventure and individualism," a sense of creating "a new world…by severing all ties with families who were left behind" (Stewart 83). This becomes a core of transnational ambiguity, for although these peoples in newlands have taken on new lives, they remain connected to families in homelands, and they continue to be involved in "family affairs" (Stewart 84). To be sure transnational connections among families creates "problems, challenges and possibilities…in extending family life across borders" (Sørensen 204). Sørensen sees that family members in such situations ask "Who migrates? Who stays behind? In what circumstances and for what purposes? What are the costs, and does this all change over time?" (from 204). Ultimately, families will experience some "losses and emotional consequences of long-distance transnational family life"

(Sørensen 205). These are all realities that transnational families must deal with, and the same can be seen in all that Stewart writes.

Families participate in filial matters including "cooperation… and… principles of intergenerational relationships" (Stewart 1). Such factors become entwined into a "changing filial ideology" (from Stewart 1). Parents do not always object to this ambiguity, much less the fact that children have decided to separate from them. One parent told Stewart, "In the era of outer-space development, it is too parochial to speak of national boundaries" (87). In similar terms, Hau states that the nation-state "[promotes] an intellectual parochialism that downplays or ignores the long history and ever-growing breadth of interaction among societies within and beyond [their] borders" (1). In any event, Stewart maintains that "loss can be overcome," and the families, children, and parents she interviewed communicated often, and connections were "not bad at all" (97). These children were often successful in their new jobs in the newlands, but that itself gave rise to ambiguous feelings and "the alienation one may feel away from one's motherland" (Stewart 99). In the newland, this alienation can creep in, and in spite of success, one worker says, "you have nowhere else to go" (Stewart 99). In spite of ongoing filial connections with parents in Taiwan, he goes on, "life here, in general, is pretty empty…you don't have too much a sense of kinship" (Stewart 99). This introduces a point that should be pondered, the ambivalence and insecurity in new lands. Perhaps this seems obvious, and Stewart found that the families she studied, though in general "very close and intimate" (100), shared feelings of ambivalence and uncertainty.

Stewart perceives a period, an era of change and challenge, for future transnational families. In this time, families will experience the potential of "joy, hope," but also of "trepidations…fear and resentment" (126). Not a few parents in these situations are "old fashioned," having grown up in different eras, the 30 s, 40 s, 50 s, and 60 s. Most parents, Stewart found, "expressed a sense of uncertainty about their future filial ties" (143). A sense of the unknown "is unanimously loud in their [tentative] narratives" (Stewart 143, 183). Many of them when they were young had had much less secure and successful jobs than their children, often proletarian, blue-collar, or working-class positions. To these people, "times have changed," although we have seen more than a few hints of how in fact they have reasonably modern views and understand the new world. At the same time, they do not want to appear out of date, and they express a "conflicting discourse" that reveals "deep-seated internal struggles and dilemmas" (Stewart 145). Ultimately, Stewart considers the "phenomenon of filial connection in a transnational context" (179), how these connections are being maintained, and what their future holds. Her answers, though always with a given ambiguity emerging from the enigmatic feelings of those in the home- and newlands in terms of how these experiences were launched, and what they held for family connections now and in the future, is fairly positive, and on the whole, it looks like all the transnational experience and character we have observed can have confident outcomes in the present day. For Taiwan, as it becomes "more of an international society," with "an increasing number of its people obtaining dual residence/citizenship, the conventional notion of a national boundary is questioned" (Stewart 189). No doubt this returns to a key point that has come up again and again in this study.

References

Academy for Cultural Diplomacy. "Chinese Diaspora Across the World: A General Overview." Accessed 21 February 2022 at https://www.culturaldiplomacy.org/academy/index.php?chinese-diaspora#:~:text=Chinese%20migrants%20amount%20to%2039.5,more%20than%2070%20million%20people.

Adachi, Nobuko, guest editor, 2010. *East Asian Transnational Migrants and Culture in a Global World. Encounters,* fall 2010.

Bannerjee, Sanjoy, Professor, San Francisco State University, personal communication with author.

Chen, Judy, 2021. "Coming Home to a Place I've Never Lived." *The News Lens,* accessed 2 January, 2022 at https://international.thenewslens.com/feature/taiwan-stories-of-return/151088.

Hau, Caroline S., Kasian Tejapira, 2011. *Traveling Nation-Makers: Transnational Flows and Movement in the Making of Modern Southeast Asia.* NUS Press, in association with Kyoto UP.

Sørensen, Ninna Nyberg 2007. *Living Across Worlds: Diaspora, Development and Transnational Engagement,*" International Organization for Migration.

Stewart. Ciloue Cheng, 2000. "Chinese American Families from Taiwan: A Transnational Study of Filial Connection." A doctoral thesis submitted to the faculty of the graduate school of the University of Minnesota.

UNESCO. "The Overseas Chinese: A long history." Located at http://corteidh.or.cr.

United Nations Department of Economic and Social Affairs (UNDESA), Population Division (2020). "International Migration 2020 Highlights"

(ST/ESA/SER.A/452). Accessed 21 March, 2022 at https://www.un.org/development/desa/pd/sites/www.un.org.development.desa.pd/files/undesa_pd_2020_international_migration_highlights.pdf.

Wikipedia, "Taiwanese People." Located at https://en.wikipedia.org/wiki/Taiwanese_people

———, "Overseas Taiwanese." Located at https://en.wikipedia.org/wiki/Overseas_Taiwanese.

———, "Overseas Chinese." Located at https://en.wikipedia.org/wiki/Overseas_Chinese#Waves_of_emigration_in_late_Qing_Dynasty.

Yeoh, Brenda S.A., Katie Willis. 2004. *State/Nation/Transnation: Perspectives on Transnationalism in the Asia-Pacific*. Routledge.

CHAPTER 6

Transnational Experience: Indigenous Peoples, Reprise

Abstract This chapter includes Taiwan indigenous peoples, of mountain and plains tribes. There are 16 tribes, with their cultures, observations, holidays and ethnic tourism. Difficulties and exploitation, and social inequality of these peoples in the past are looked at. Modern improvements and associations and groups working to rectify this are examined. Indigenous embrace of Taiwanese nationality, and relation to ancient Out of Taiwan developments are viewed. Examination of indigenous holidays and observations, with commentary by Taiwanese indigenous person Sayun Tosu, on these facts. Within the indigenous celebrations, we see native Taiwan peoples honoring and observing their ancestors, often in oceanic contexts, related to the Out of Taiwan in ages past.

Keywords Taiwan indigenous peoples · Tribes · Tribal observations and holidays · Sayun Tosu · Out of Taiwan · Tourism · Ethnic tourism · Injustice · Inequality

Let's take a look at the already mentioned indigenous peoples who currently live in Taiwan. These are the descendants of the peoples who once launched the transnational Out of Taiwan explorations, and in the present day, they carry such a worldview in their consciousness.

D. Pendery, *Transnational Taiwan*,
https://doi.org/10.1007/978-981-19-4368-3_6

Currently, there are 16 officially recognized indigenous tribes in Taiwan: Amis (a fishing culture, attached to the ocean), Atayal (also called Tayal), Paiwan, Bunun, Puyuma (also called Pinuyumayan), Rukai, Tsou, Saisiyat, Yami (dwelling on Orchid Island, and also called Tao), Thao, Kavalan, Truku, Sakizaya, Sediq, Hla'alua, and Kanakanavu. These tribes are found in mountainous and plains regions, on coasts and islands, and a number of other groups are awaiting recognition. These groups now number about 569,000 people, or 2.38% of the island's population, though the number rises significantly if unrecognized groups are included.

Research has shown that the ancestors of these peoples have been living in Taiwan for at least 6,500 years, though some research extends much farther into the past than this. Most of the first ancestors of Taiwan's aboriginal tribes came from China. As seen in the Out of Taiwan thesis, however, these peoples have long-running linguistic and cultural ties and connections not only with the Chinese people, but as well with Austronesian peoples in the Philippines, Micronesia, Indonesia, Malaysia, Brunei, East Timor, Madagascar, and Polynesia.

For centuries, Taiwan's indigenous peoples have experienced economic exploitation and social and military conflict with colonizing powers, including the Dutch, Spanish, to some extent the Chinese, and the Japanese. The colonizers pressured native peoples into cultural assimilation and the adoption of often ill-fitting new lifestyles, as well as inter-marriage with the intruders. A great deal of "language shift" (the process in which members of a community abandon their original vernacular or language in favor of another) and language death has occurred. Of the approximately 26 known languages of the Taiwanese indigenous peoples, at least ten are now extinct, five are moribund, and several are to some degree endangered.

Taiwan's indigenous peoples have traditionally been known as the "mountain" and "plains" peoples, and to a great extent they still live in these areas, although a significant portion now live in urban areas. To what extent this has altered their traditional cultures, and not least their ocean-going practices, may be an area of debate. In any event, it is their traditional festivals, rituals, and other practices that draw the attention of many ordinary Taiwanese, as well as visitors and tourists in Taiwan, and which in turn contribute to a true transnational interconnection and dialog. I will return to this observation below.

Of course, the Taiwan indigenous peoples are natives of Taiwan, and they very much adopt and embrace a Taiwanese "nationality." In this sense, they are in the "here and now," and this nation is very much their home and birthright, and it could be said that they are simply "national" and not truly "transnational." But this is not the reality. Although they may not be traveling as often to newlands (whether by sea or other means) as they once did, with their heritage and background, their forebears and ancestors, the Taiwan indigenous people continue to evince a feel of the traveler, the migrant, the expatriate introducing and adopting new cultures into their own and other cultures (and we will see more how this is true in Taiwan today, below). They will always have this, "nations" of their own, and in some such ways they introduce and foster transnational attitudes in life to this day, as they interact with Taiwanese and other peoples.

The indigenous peoples of Taiwan have experienced a great deal of economic and social inequality, which has resulted in high unemployment, some problems with alcohol consumption, broken families, and substandard education. In recent decades, indigenous groups have actively sought a higher degree of political self-determination and economic development, and this has in large part been accomplished in Taiwan. In December 1984, the Taiwan Aboriginal People's Movement was created when aboriginal political activists and the Presbyterian Church in Taiwan established the Alliance of Taiwan Aborigines (ATA), in order to highlight the problems experienced by indigenous communities. In the late 1980s, a "Return Our Land Movement" (還我土地, Huán wǒ tǔdì, Return my land) was launched, in which aborigines stipulated the return of lands to aboriginal inhabitants, and the ATA sent a representative to the United Nations (UN) Working Group on Indigenous Populations.

The Taiwan government and indigenous peoples created a "New Partnership Between the Indigenous Peoples and the Government of Taiwan" in 2002, article 1 of which affirms that "the government shall recognize the inherent sovereignty of Taiwan's indigenous peoples," while article 2 stipulates that "the government shall promote and implement the indigenous self-government" (Mona 88). This new partnership announced it "would structure its relations with indigenous peoples on a [very much transnational] 'Nation-to-Nation' basis" (Mona 85). Aboriginal Taiwanese have also sought to have the Republic of China constitution reworded to ensure indigenous "dignity and justice" in the form of enhanced legal protection, government assistance, and the right to identify themselves as 原住民 (yuán zhù mín, the people who lived here first) (from Wikipedia, "Taiwanese indigenous peoples").

Taiwan's Council of Indigenous Peoples was established in 1996, seeking autonomy, recognition, and extended rights and privileges for Taiwan's indigenous peoples. Soon after this, aboriginal languages were more widely used and taught in schools, and this movement has taken on great importance in Taiwan. "The present political leaders in the aboriginal community…have been effective in leveraging their ethnic identity and socio-linguistic acculturation into contemporary Taiwanese society," and all of this has introduced a given transnationalism into Taiwanese life, with new languages, peoples, and cultures coming into view, in contrast with various other nationalities and political leanings (from Wikipedia, "Taiwanese indigenous peoples"). August 1 has now been designated Indigenous Peoples day in Taiwan.

A number of other government groups, departments, and councils, as well as many formed independently by Taiwanese people, focus on indigenous groups, their development, families, education, and employment. Efforts are under way in indigenous communities to revive traditional cultural practices and preserve their traditional languages, and as noted to observe traditional holidays, festivals, and other cultural activities. Along this line, a given transnationalism is evinced by way of their involvement in "ethnic tourism" activities and their formal observations of various native holidays, celebrations, and festivals. Even eco-tourism has been practiced, with various native farms around the island hosting activities and stay-overs for tourists. The same is true in terms of music and sports activities, and a given revival of aboriginal pride and increased cultural activity has been seen in Taiwan, with the indigenous peoples overlapping into and interacting with other cultures. Let's look at some of the indigenous holidays and festivals, some of which, perhaps most importantly, focus on oceanic and maritime expeditions, as well as celebrations of antecedents and ancestors, with their links to Out of Taiwan (much below from the Taiwan Council of Indigenous Peoples, the Hualien Indigenous Peoples Department, and the Tourism Bureau, Republic of China).

Taitung City (臺東市) in Taiwan has launched an indigenous festival that seems perfectly in keeping with Out of Taiwan, the Austronesian Cultural Festival, which highlights Austronesian navigational culture, and the ties between indigenous peoples in Taiwan and the Asia–Pacific region. The festival looks at "the close relationship between Austronesian people and the ocean—where they find their food, go adventuring and trade in goods or crafts with other islands," said Taitung County Commissioner Hsu Ching-yuan (徐慶元) (from Mao).

The Amis people (阿美族), with an estimated population of 52,395, and as noted the most populous indigenous tribe in Taiwan, celebrate a Fishing or Catch Festival, held between June and August. An Ocean God and other deities are recognized and worshipped, and sacrifices are made to ensure good traveling conditions. One such sacrifice, Asan Surot told me, takes place "when a storm is brewing," and then "a white chicken is sacrificed to the ocean, to mediate and make accord with white caps on the waves, and ensure good weather."

The Catch includes a sea ritual and a river ritual to thank the sea and river deities, and to ensure good catches in the "new fishing year." The Amis pray for peace on the sea/river and a high catch. "That's why we stayed," Surot told me, "because the fisheries were better." The ceremony begins with the worship of the river deity or sea deity. Amis of different ages fish, and young people gather and cook the catch and distribute it to Amis according to their seniority. In return, the elderly will share the catch with young people to express the concepts of sharing and respect for the elderly. In addition, The Amis also celebrate an Ocean Festival, a traditional ceremony where they pray for safe fishing and abundant catches. This festival is "serious," says Sayun Tosu, an Atayal indigenous person working as an Executive Officer for International Affairs at the Taiwan Council of Indigenous Peoples. "It has specific processes," she says, by which "the Amis honor their ancient ocean-going ancestors, which is in contrast to the common media portrayals of singing, dancing, drinking festivals in Taiwan."

Tosu tells me that the Amis "are striving to revitalize their ocean-going culture, by building craft, honing navigation skills, and returning to the sea hunts, which have long been their main food supply." The Amis people "are learning from and communicating with other Pacific island nations" in their efforts, she adds.

The Kavalan (噶瑪蘭族), a very small tribe estimated at 640, also celebrate an Ocean Festival during the change from spring to summer in March and April. This tribe, once ocean-going, do not pursue this lifestyle as often today. Kavalan men select an auspicious day and gather by the sea. In the morning, the elders make offerings to the ancestors and then the young men head out fishing. Around noon, the fishermen return to the greeting of the elders. The fresh catch is cooked with vegetables by the sea, and some fish is sent back to the village to share with those who were unable to attend.

Fishermen in southern Taiwan aboriginal communities observe the Burning of the Plague God Boat festival. The original purpose of this ritual was to send the Plague God out to sea, taking disease and pestilence with him. Today, it has become an activity to solicit peace and good fortune. According to custom, in the boat-burning celebration, a fire is set by devotees as other participants prepare goods for the symbolic trip. Then a large bonfire is made in order to force out any bad spirits, the Plague God boards, and the boat is burned as the devotees pray for peace.

The Yami tribe performs an Ocean festival, and several "flying fish" rituals and festivals, indicating their ocean-based culture. Orchid Island is known by this island-dwelling people as *Ma'ataw* ("floating in the sea").

The Tao also observe a Launching Ritual, in which a ship and crew set out to ensure good health and the smooth voyage of the craft. The crew wears formal clothing and boards the ship, after which the captain knocks the stern keel and the first deck to enable good luck. Then, the captain makes a hole on the stern keel, and seals the hole to pray for the health and longevity of the crew and good luck for the voyage.

Most of all the tribes in Taiwan celebrate festivals honoring ancestors. The Kavalan tribe celebrates a year-end Ancestral Spirit Ritual, the Palilin Festival, usually held by individual families. Ancestors including the female or male head of the house, and deceased relatives on both sides of the family are honored. The Sakizaya (撒奇萊雅族) observe their Palamal Fire God Festival, to express remembrance of ancestors (these people were once ocean-going, Tosu tells me, but this is much less common today). The people attempt to restore original identity and reunite with ancestors, and the younger generations are trained to preserve the bloodline flowing in their veins. The Atayal (泰雅) have an Ancestral Spirit Ritual called Maho, the Pinuyumayan (卑南族) have a Patrilineal Ancestral Shrine, and the Saisiyat (賽夏) hold a ceremony of ancestral spirits (paSbaki'), a ceremony in which ancestral spirits are seen as the principal forces of tribal protection, affecting good and bad fortune in daily life. The Pinuyumayan also have an ancestral ritual venue, while the Amis' Catch event is an event showing respect for the elderly and the tribal sages.

In all of the above celebrations, we see native Taiwan peoples honoring and observing their ancestors, often in oceanic contexts, harking back to the Out of Taiwan migrations that spread a new transnationality across the Indo-Pacific region in ages past.

References

Mao, Huan-wen, 2005. "Event celebrates seafaring culture," *Taipei Times,* 4 August, 2005. Located at https://www.taipeitimes.com/News/taiwan/archives/2005/08/04/2003266339.

Mona, Awi, 2007. "International Perspective on the Constitutionality of Indigenous Peoples' Rights," *Taiwan International Studies Quarterly*, 3.2, Summer: 85–139. Accessed 21 February, 2022 at http://tisanet.org/quarterly/3-2-4.pdf.

Hualien Indigenous Peoples Department. Located at https://ab.hl.gov.tw/en-us/Home/Index.

Taiwan Council of Indigenous Peoples. Located at https://www.cip.gov.tw/en/index.html.

Tourism Bureau, Republic of China, https://eng.taiwan.net.tw.

Tosu, Sayun, 28 March, 2022. Personal interview with employee at the Taiwan Council of Indigenous Peoples.

Wikipedia. "Orchid Island." Located at https://en.wikipedia.org/wiki/Orchid_Island.

———, "Taiwanese indigenous peoples." Located at https://en.wikipedia.org/wiki/Taiwanese_indigenous_peoples.

CHAPTER 7

Transnational Governance

Abstract Transnational government policies and procedures are examined, with multidirectional interplays and interactions in populations comprised of both local citizens and traveling foreigners. Reduction of sovereign state behavior and diplomacy is seen, in these lights. Individuals are playing key roles in governance now, with transnational and local civil society and social movements in development. Taiwan's approach to climate change sees these developments. Global transnational governance and new international legal regimes are weakening, impacting the state as the only legitimate source of rights. Transnational governance is viewed as a regulated arena. The Asian-focused Regional Comprehensive Economic Partnership and transnational agreements are looked at. Reduction of state sovereignty is being seen. "Experts," "Statist" and "Community" modes of governance are examined. Introduction of Non-state Actors into transnational governance, along with NGOs, multi- and transnational corporations, epistemic communities, and social and liberation movements. Taiwan President Tsai Ing-wen's New Southbound Policy as a transnational network development is looked at. Asian think tanks as carriers of these ideas. Taiwan warm power and interactions with India.

Keywords Transnational governance · Sovereign state power · Climate change · Government regulation · Expert · Statist and Community

D. Pendery, *Transnational Taiwan*,
https://doi.org/10.1007/978-981-19-4368-3_7

governance · NGOs · Transnational corporations · Social movements · President Tsai Ing-wen · New Southbound Policy · Asian think tanks

To move ahead, some of the above may suggest a look at transnational governance, and the steps that states are taking to deal with this phenomenon, in populations comprised of both local citizens and traveling foreigners. This is to ask, in terms of transnational individuals and their travels and challenges, what exactly will the transnational state be comprised of, what will be its functions, responsibilities, contextual setting, and shape? We have already considered the state itself, its many guises, and whether it will continue to exist or not, and so we leave that question aside here. Held et al. observe a significant impact on governance—"decisional, institutional, distributional and structural" elements—in the shifting nation-state, with the advent of transnational migration. These authors note demographic changes that are "altering the composition and size of the population" of both source and recipient countries (313), and impacting the "provision of welfare services, housing and education as well as the operation of the economy itself" (313). They observe that the flow of illegal immigrants (these have not been our focus, admittedly), demonstrates the limited capacity of many nation-states to secure independently their own borders. This introduces a "changing nature of state autonomy and sovereignty and the necessity to increase transborder cooperation" (321–322). Further, "the collective strength and pattern of alliances…has changed, and migration has reshaped political interest and perceptions" (322). Finally, "migration has altered the kinds of policy options available to states and the balance of costs and benefits that those policies bear" (322). We see substantive governmental changes behind the scenes here.

Such governance "is characterized in our transnational world by intense activity and activism, by dense and multidirectional interplays and interactions" (Djelic 390). States, as we have noted, will still exist in this field, but they are "only one type of actor among others," and are not "the central mainsprings of the re-governing process" (Djelic 4). Transnational governance indicates that "governance activity is embedded in particular geopolitical structures and hence enveloped in multiple and interacting institutional webs" with ambiguous "interdependence and entanglement" (Djelic 4). Such an "uncertain" view will be very much in accordance with the views of Stephen Toulmin, to be examined below.

When we speak of global governance, we no longer mean simply sovereign state-to-state diplomacy, international treaties, or intergovernmental organizations like the UN. Alongside these (call them "traditional") elements of global politics are many new institutions, fluctuating across global networks comprising governmental officials, business persons, and private citizens, all with given codes of conduct, mandates, rules, and canons. We view a network, a labyrinth of governmental and intergovernmental organizations, MNCs and other businesses, operational partnerships, NGOs, non-state actors (NSAs) other transnational actors, and of course all the individuals, politicians and citizens that interact in these contexts. This is to say that within these circuitries, individuals play key roles, with transnational and local civil society and social movements coming into play. These mechanisms and alliances offer exciting solutions to pressing transnational challenges as diverse as climate change, financial administration, workers' rights, and public health. But they also raise new questions about the effectiveness and legitimacy of transnational governance—that is, the situations and problems outside the usual limits of corporate or governmental hierarchies, which present new challenges to all of the groups and peoples we have considered. In all of this, we seek to understand and implement processes measuring how transnational institutions conduct public affairs, manage public resources and guarantee the realization of human rights in a manner free of abuse and corruption, with due regard for the rule of law. Transnational, like any governance, is "the process of decision-making and the process by which decisions are implemented (or not implemented)" (from UN-ESCAP). Transnational governance here can apply to corporate, international, national, or local governance, as well as the interactions between other sectors of society.

We will see all of this in terms of Taiwan, going forward, and indeed, all of the above multiplicity can be seen in Taiwan's approach to climate change. Although Taiwan had long focused on a "sovereignty-centered approach" to this problem, with attention wholly on "the state" and various state-centered methods, more recently it has adopted a "polycentric climate regime, which includes many different actors and methods in the private, public, and epistemic communities" (Biedermann 25). Taiwan's adoption of such methods includes "commitment to the Paris Agreement, plans for comprehensive unilateral measures, participation in transparency institutions, financial market mechanisms, and taking bilateral as well as multilateral approaches," all efforts that harken the transnational (Biedermann 25). More specifically, Taipei the city, employing a transnational governance mode, "applies a multidimensional strategy" in its anti-pollution efforts, which "includes NGOs, corporations, diplomatic allies, and initiatives at the both regional and national level" (Biedermann 43). "Taipei strives for leadership in climate mitigation policies as an APEC member," and in sum this multi-layered approach, "may make the country a leader in this field in East Asia" (Biedermann 25). We will continue to look more at Taiwan transnational governance, below.

Global transnational transformations and new international legal regimes have weakened the state as the only legitimate source of rights, much less sovereignty, and such formulations are of growing importance. It is said that decolonization and the fall of communism led to a growing status of human rights in most nations and has forced states to take account of "persons qua persons," rather than "persons qua citizens." As a result, individuals have rights and freedoms regardless of their citizenship status within a country, and this is no doubt most true in terms of transnational persons.

Transnational governance is a highly regulated arena, perhaps because of the complexity and diversity of the many actors involved, and the fact that states, though of a reduced role and impact ("weakened" some say) continue to play a prominent role. As one example, we might look at given treaties signed by states, and see, particularly when the treaty involves a number of nations, a very-much transnational (and essentially liberalizing) action. The Comprehensive and Progressive Agreement for Trans-Pacific Partnership comes to mind, a trade agreement signed by Australia, Brunei, Canada, Chile, Japan, Malaysia, Mexico, New Zealand, Peru, Singapore, and Vietnam (needless to say the United States withdrew from the original agreement under Donald Trump). Taiwan has expressed strong interest in joining this group, has implemented domestic reforms to improve its chances, and is being considered at this time. The agreement contains certain governance actions, such as reducing corruption and compliance with UN requirements for effective and uncorrupt legal regimes and administration. It also seeks to abide by human rights expectations and norms, further "transnationalizing" the agreement. The Asian-focused Regional Comprehensive Economic Partnership, comprising Australia, Brunei, Cambodia, China, Indonesia,

Japan, South Korea, Laos, Malaysia, Myanmar, New Zealand, the Philippines, Singapore, Thailand, and Vietnam could be seen in the same light, and no doubt we could look at any number of other such agreements, in areas of trade, borders, environmental and scientific research, weapons, media, diversity, and human equality. These treaties in essence depend a great deal on sovereign nation-state status, but at the same time are very much transnationalizing agreements, as can be seen in their (generally) collegial qualities and the way they bring peoples together in cooperative contracts. And to be sure in addition to nation-states proper, these and other treaties often include individuals, business entities, and other legal entities. In this sense, the conception goes beyond just treaties, and into a variety of other international agreements, protocols, covenants, conventions, pacts, memorandums of understanding, or exchanges of letters. Though a bit different than the concrete measures outlined above, the presence of a number of transnational think tanks in Taiwanese academic, social, and governmental circles indicates a roughly similar sort of rule- and accord-making, and like efforts toward agreement on principle and practice. More on this just below.

In a word, a given "governance" is required, though we have seen already that this is by no means always "state" governance. A sometimes-equivocal field of actors, institutions, and spaces or spheres emerges in this conception. In terms of such actors, and given that economic considerations instill themselves so firmly in all of these relations, MNCs and other businesses, as well as their employees, are no doubt key. These actors instigate many of the communal relations that play a central role in transnationalism, not least in term of laws, rules, regulations, and agreements that are formulated to control and manage these connections, which are in general created and enforced across various spaces, national and otherwise. The impact of that which is truly "national"—the rules and regulations actually formulated by various states/bureaucratic/legislative actors and enforced within state structures—often comes into play here, creating quite a bit of complexity and conflict. At the same time, transnational actors are seeing the rise of "distinctive emergent properties from the actions of public and private actors across diverse national contexts and across diverse spatial levels" (Djelic 143).[1] Other actors are found

[1] Djelic and Sahlin-Andersson describe transnational firms as being pulled in various directions, from the strictly national, to the corporate, to the local, which is in sum a

in the fields of defense, labor, NGOs, and other NSAs, various international organizations, media, banking, higher education, health care, public management and, of course, actual nation-states and associated regulators themselves. All of these entities engage in "governance capacity…dispersed among and shared between many actors," and all are "increasingly governed in similar ways—transnationally" (Djelic 248).

Djelic and Sahlin-Andersson see an "emergent and stabilizing order" in all of this (390), and a "rich pool of actors concerned with and to a greater or lesser degree involved in governance" (392). Within this "multiplicity" is "evidence of significant progressive convergence" (392). At the highest level, "The existence of a governance issue fosters the emergence and development of a governance network," but "the structuration of a network can also transform a particular, often limited project into a transnational governance issue" (Djelic 393).

Djelic and Sahlin-Andersson visualize three spheres or scenarios for transnational governance. In the "Experts" scenario, the "rule makers" are generally (though not always) separated from the "rule followers." As "experts' in fields, they have the credibility, legitimacy, and ability to make the rules. The rule followers (seemingly groups of migrant workers, primarily) are in "awe" of the rule makers, because of their know-how. There is no true power of coercion by the rule makers to control the followers, as they are not "governmental" in the true sense. In this respect, this is less transnational governance than it first appears. In the second scenario, the rule makers are "Statists," that is individuals with the power of the state to make and enforce law. Again, these rule makers are wholly separate from the followers, existing in the clouds of state government power as it were. The rule making process is political, in the classic sense, which may include the input of both "experts" and "followers." Actual coercion and constraint are the ways in which rules are enforced, and though this may take place across given transnational institutions and

"differentiated and interdependent network…integrated with a flexible coordinating mechanism" combined with "cross-national leaning" (141). What emerges as transnational is a new actor where the dominance of single national origin and associated state-centric practices and processes is no longer the defining feature (reworded from page 141). Though criticized by some, this view "suggests that the firm has the power to coordinate effectively its members across different national spaces, to enable them to learn from differences across contexts, to implant this learning within is procedures to produce new improved practices and to reproduce these capabilities over the long term as individuals move in and out of the organization" (142).

groupings, this all looks a lot like standard state-centered power. The third "Community" scenario no doubt indicates the true possibility of transnational, networked power-sharing and in turn communal relations, economic associations and, at the highest level, government communion. In this sphere, rule makers and rule followers are a collaborative enterprise. The mode and logic of this approach is that of negotiation, "with the ultimate objective of reaching a saturation of 'communion'" (Djelic 305). What such communal government seeks "before anything else, are common beliefs" (Djelic 305). With all of this, "standards, norms and practices should follow all the more naturally and easily" and are in effect, a type of "socialization," "self-regulation," and "self-responsibilization" (as opposed to coercion and constraints) (Djelic 305-06). Ultimately, just such a transnational social space will "become increasingly widespread" in the future (Djelic 305).

In addition to all of the above, we should note the ideal, conception and practice of NSAs in national and global governance. Such actors can be very prominent and important in national and international affairs and can include NGOs, multi- and transnational corporations, epistemic communities (networks of experts on certain policy issues), social and liberation movements, churches, and criminal networks. Looking at NSAs (or, alternatively "transnational advocacy networks" [from Arts, 8]), we can in essence view participants as transnational entities, impacting both international organizations and specific states, in the terms and conceptions outlined throughout this work. Looking at NSAs and their cooperation with other groups and entities, Arts asks whether "non-state actors do matter in international and foreign politics" (8). "Proponents of *state*-centric approaches tend to believe that they do not" he says (8, italics in original), whereas "proponents of society-centered approaches tend to believe that they do" (8). Yet further, in fact, "It may be that NSAs are becoming more important than states as initiators of change," though "system change ultimately happens *through* states" (8, italics in original). And we will see more of Taiwan's interactions with NSAs just below. In that sense [and as we have seen], "states still are at the center of the international system" (Wendt in Arts 8). But Arts counters this, writing "Society-centered approaches [we have seen that these are in essence transnational] have challenged these claims" (Arts 9, with added text). They have "broadened the concept of international politics, have referred to the spectacular rise in the number of non-state actors in the international arena since World War II, and have argued that non-state actors may be initiators of fundamental change and that they may even overrule governments" (Arts 9). And in turn, commentators have seen that "the transnational debate has remained too state-centric, defining politics and non-state actors merely in terms of the nation-state, thus neglecting the social dimension of politics and transnational actors" (Arts 9). Overall, we find that states and NSAs often work together, but they are working in transnational contexts and on transnational issues. To be sure in all of this we are witnessing a variety of clashing meta-theoretical worldviews, theories, notions of power, policies and practices, and experiential analyses. Where does Taiwan stand? Some note that Taiwan's engagement with NSAs has found newfound importance in terms of President Tsai Ing-wen's New Southbound Policy (NSP), which has extended Taiwan's reach in economics, politics, social affairs and education to a number of SE Asian nations. Kabinawa has emphasized how Taiwan has increased its incorporation of NSAs into its foreign policy. This can be seen as a move away from state-centered power, as opposed to Taiwan's authoritarian past (which of course focused almost wholly on state-centered power). Taiwan is now utilizing greater cooperation with NSAs, and in the main reduced state-to-state diplomacy in world affairs.[2] The nation has adopted a new ardency in working with NSAs and developed sets of new policy initiatives to operate in these ways.

To continue, and still with Taiwan in mind, the NSP has promoted a vibrant new multiculturalism, connecting the various countries involved, and has implemented new policy programs to increase the number of Southeast Asians living, working, and studying in Taiwan (and the reverse, Taiwanese people doing these things in SE Asian countries). And Taiwan has taken further steps and engaged with a number of think tanks across borders (certainly such think tanks and their policy-implementing activities are among the most important transnational NSAs), creating "cross-border networks of society between Taiwan and Southeast Asia" (Kabinawa, no page number). In these lights, the Taiwan-Asia Exchange Foundation (TAEF) is a policy-oriented think tank focusing on SE Asian affairs establishing cooperative partnerships with the SE Asian nations. The TAEF is encouraging ties among NSAs, including think tanks, NGOs, and youth leaders from Taiwan and other SE Asian countries.

[2] Some may disagree with this statement, and indicate how in fact Taiwan remains very much state-centered in its efforts to maintain diplomatic ties and increase cooperation with other states. To be sure this is true, and I will refer again to this view.

Another think tank to work in these areas is the Taiwan NextGen Foundation, a not-for-profit education foundation/think tank that aims to "unlock the value and talents of grass-roots movements" (Taiwan NextGen). Additionally, the Taiwan Fellowship provides for research into Asian topics, with connection to international opinion leaders, academic relations and the internationalization of education, and cultural and public diplomacy. In the end, Taiwan's transnational efforts in these areas and with these entities has helped the nation to "promote democracy and its national identity in the region, improve Taiwan's visibility in Southeast Asia, and generate solidarity with its Southeast Asian counterparts" (from Kabinawa). Others have also observed how NSAs, including media, think tanks, and other organizations have "played a crucial role in forging closer ties between Taiwan and India" (Gill, no page number), such as the bilateral transnational development program spearheaded by the TAEF, in which the TAEF and India's National Maritime Foundation signed a memorandum of understanding to deepen Taiwan-India cooperation in maritime affairs and regional development. The TAEF has itself launched a number of other programs, including the Asian Double Helix Project, to collaborate with Asian institutions in order to develop social innovation and public governance talents, and a Civil Society Connectivity program, focusing on local communication networks in Asian civil society, talent incubation, issue advocacy, and the deepening of capacity building projects. The TAEF says this "will strengthen Taiwan's 'warm power' in Asian countries" (TAEF).

In all of the above we see that Taiwan has made important public moves to work with transnational actors of all sorts, not least those participating in non-state activities. Now let's take a yet-closer look at Taiwan's transnational governance.

References

Arts, Bas, 2003. "Non-state Actors in Global Governance: Three Faces of Power." Preprints aus der Max-Planck-Projektgruppe Recht der Gemeinschaftsgüter, No. 2003/4, Max-Planck-Projektgruppe Recht der Gemeinschaftsgüter, Bonn. Accessed 31 January 2022 at https://www.econstor.eu/bitstream/10419/85112/1/2003-04_online.pdf.

Biedermann, Reinhard, 2017. "Taiwan's Polycentric Strategy Within the Environmental Regime Complex on Climate Change." *ASIEN 143* (April 2017),

S. 25–46. Located at http://asienforschung.de/wp-content/uploads/2018/03/143_RA_Biedermann_ClimateChange_final.pdf.

Djelic, Marie-Laure, Kerstin Sahlin-Andersson, eds., 2006. *Transnational Governance: Institutional Dynamics of Regulation*. Cambridge UP.

Gill, Don Maclain, 2020. "The Role of Non-state Actors in Forging Closer India-Taiwan Relations." *Taiwan Insight*. Accessed 12 March 2022 at https://taiwaninsight.org/2020/10/20/the-role-of-non-state-actors-in-forging-closer-india-taiwan-relations/.

Held, David, Anthony McGrew, David Goldblatt, Jonathan Perraton, 1999. *Global Transformations: Politics, Economics, and Culture*. Polity Press.

Kabinawa, Ratih, 2021. "Bringing Back Transnational Relations: Non-State Actors in Taiwan's New Southbound Policy." *Taiwan Insight*, 22 April. Accessed 15 March 2022 at https://taiwaninsight.org/2021/04/22/bringing-back-transnational-relations-non-state-actors-in-taiwans-new-southbound-policy/.

Taiwan Asia Exchange Foundation (TAEF). Accessed 1 March 2022 at https://www.taef.org/about.

Taiwan NextGen Foundation. "Empowering the Next Generation of Taiwan's Leaders." Accessed 15 March, 2022 at https://en.taiwannextgenfoundation.org/about.

UN-ESCAP. "What Is Good Governance?" Accessed 17 February 2022 at http://www.gdrc.org/u-gov/escap-governance.htm.

CHAPTER 8

Taiwan and Transnational Governance

Abstract Taiwan's free democracy viewed as a method of transnational governance is examined, as well as reduction of state-centered governance and sovereignty. The UN is seen as a simultaneous transnational and state-centered entity. Existence of NSAs NGOs, multinational firms, international organizations, and individuals as transnational governance entities, using "softer" governmental mechanisms. Move in governance from public to private, hard to soft, state-centric to socially based, hierarchical and enforced to open and networked. Taiwan's open society and technological development could make a move in this direction. Taiwan as "non-transnational" nation, retaining state-centered focus on power and governance. Hugues Mignot,, Belgium's top representative to Taiwan, is cited. China's suppression of Taiwan reducing Taiwan's overall transnational existence, and Taiwan and China's recognition of a transnational existence that links the two countries. Taiwan's recognition of the "states" of its indigenous peoples as a transnational take in affairs. David Pendery's "New Approach to Diplomatic Bind" with a look at statehood, governance, and recognition in these lights. Introduction of the *Union Mondiale*, Global Union, with "world citizens." Introduction of "cosmopolitan democracy," possible transnational understanding, by David Held. Taiwan as a "true transnational state" (Pendery), and Taiwan's social movements and other actions in Taiwan as elements of this. A return to the Taiwan diaspora, and transnational participation by Taiwanese actors.

D. Pendery, *Transnational Taiwan*,
https://doi.org/10.1007/978-981-19-4368-3_8

Keywords Taiwan transnational governance · State-centric power and reduction · NSAs NGOs · Multinational firms · International organizations · Individuals · China · Hugues Mignot · *Union Mondiale* · World citizen · Cosmopolitan democracy · Taiwan social movements · Diaspora

In all of the above we have seen conceptions and constructions of transnational governance (and perhaps to some extent, "non-governance"). Are they true and applicable in Taiwan? Well at the various individual and non-state levels looked at above, we have already seen that this is true. Further, at the highest level, Taiwan's free, democracy, political rights, civil liberties, observation of the rule of law, political pluralism, and freedom of expression indicate just such a possibility—that is, a "state" fully liberal, participatory and cooperative in its governmental efforts, no doubt trans/international in scope. To be sure all the citizens of Taiwan have the freedom to participate in governance, and you could take this a step further and say that a small number of foreigners with actual Taiwan citizenship, as well as a goodly number of alien "residents," also have a fair stake in governance here. What may result is "bridges spanning nations and transnational communities," which may "enable…democratizing potentials…truly global in scope" (Sørensen 200). And so, in this sense symbiotic democracy itself, always inviting citizens and others to participate, seems to be a paragon of transnational governance. To be sure transnational governance in Taiwan and elsewhere is a step back from a realist, "state-centered" approach to polity, lawmaking, civic life, and statecraft in the large sense. One cannot now neatly theorize the state as sovereign, absolute, necessarily autonomous, or even, in some senses, "self-governing." The reality of transnational actors involved in the polities of a nation, with all the possible border crossings and networked connectivity this entails, indicates that the status of the state as fully in charge of all of its affairs seems a stretch, and a multiply connected (and in effect multiply administered and overseen) new entity is in place now. Now, as noted above, this may not be fully applicable to Taiwan at this time—the "state" of Taiwan/Republic of China has made great efforts to be recognized as just this, and nothing else, and this very state-centered approach to governance and politics is very troublesome in terms of our argument. Needless to say, Taiwan/Republic of China has sought admission into the UN for years as a "state"—that and nothing more. At a high level, some would argue that the UN is in effect a transnational institution that has sought to bring the peoples of the world together into a networked approach to polity, governance and international affairs. But the fact remains that the UN is very much a "state centered" organization, and time and again it has made it clear that states and only states will be granted admission. Related to this is the concept of state-to-state recognition, an area that Taiwan has also been ensconced in for decades.[1] To say it again, this approach to politics is very much antithetical to the transnational approach, and Taiwan's immersion in this method is problematic.

To continue this discussion, it is said that "Transnational governance typically involves non-state actors as principals, as nongovernmental organizations (NGOs), multinational firms, international organizations, and many individuals respond to problems that cross-national jurisdictions—often in the absence of meaningful involvement by national governments" (Bevir, no page number). It can be seen here that Taiwan, likely, has just such connectivity with the actors noted, not least a number of NSAs, NGOs, and international organizations (and that could even include the UN). In these ways, there are fewer attachments to state-centered powers, proper, and there is indeed a more transnational form of administration, lawmaking, and out-and-out governance. Further, transnational governance "does not impose formal international institutional authority on states, but rather uses 'softer' mechanisms" in order to meet "a relevant set of broadly consensual standards" (Bevir, no page number). Though it may be a stretch to say that such laws and regulations "have no legally binding force," the essential idea that such laws and regulations are more "socially constructed" (as opposed to put into force by public officials) holds true. Sørensen goes so far as to say this sort of regulation is in the main "voluntary" (377), and "open…to negotiation and translations by those who are regulated" (378) which may shed some light on the overall concept. Such "softer" approaches should be considered, and we may see

[1] I probably don't need to mention here that Taiwan's "state-to-state" relations in the diplomatic world of such recognition, have taken a serious hit in the last several years under President Tsai Ing-wen, and the nation has lost eight diplomatic allies, including Burkina Faso, Panama, Sao Tome and Principe, Dominican Republic, El Salvador, Solomon Islands, Kiribati, and recently Nicaragua.

a difference emerge from state-centered "government," toward transnational "governance," which I think Taiwan may find itself on the verge of.

Governance, in a word, "rests upon multiple authorities that are not necessarily public" (Sørensen 123), "public" here meaning state-authorized and supported personnel. Such public actors will play a role, but they will work with transnational people and groups, NSAs, NGOs, and the like. And it will be these people and groups that engage in soft law and regulation, which are a lot less coercive than standard conceptions of such controls. Such a governance will be "societally based" (Sørensen 124), as "issues change and require more participation form ordinary [transnational] people" (Sørensen 124), reducing reliance on hierarchical, standards, much less state-centered democratic models. "[S]ocial sanctions and processes of socialization are viewed as powerful compliance mechanisms" here (Sørensen 124), indicating the sociality, the communality, the collectivity of this model. Here, I am broadly considering the work of Paul Hirst, who has shown that the makings of traditional democracy in state-centered, hierarchical, party-centric conditions is now out of step with the transnational world. He aims to "re-organize democracy from the state to voluntary and democratically self-governing associations" (Sørensen 126). To sum up, in all of these modes of "governance" as opposed to "government," the moves are from public to private, from hard to soft, from state-centric to socially based, from hierarchical and enforced to open and networked. Though this might not be specifically at work in Taiwan today, I have a feeling that Taiwan's somewhat open- and open-minded society could make a move in this direction, and we may see a transfer into a given "ideational power" structure. I might well note here that Taiwan has some 200 political parties (most probably officially endorsed by the state), which to be sure indicates a freer, more open, collective, multiple structure of governance and electoral choice (from Wikipedia, "List of political parties in Taiwan").

In some senses, and this is to repeat, simply the fact of Taiwan's free, open, liberal, egalitarian democracy can be seen in these lights, and the nation's politics and polity have been recognized as technologically, and in the main, communally, innovative (in fact Taiwan's use of a vote-counting system, as opposed to the United States' electoral college, has been praised as an innovative approach that might have a broader impact in the future). Digital tools encouraging citizen participation in democracy, for example, "have become a fundamental part of Taiwan's political system, making it one of the most innovative democracies worldwide" (Hierlemann, no page number). Taiwan has introduced a number of such technological-democratic moves, bringing technology into the spaces where citizens can employ "open-data solutions" in their access to governmental functions, and in their petitions and impact on government policy and regulation. Social and political movements in Taiwan (the Sunflower Movement, etc.) have widely used digital technology and social networks to spread their message. Audrey Tang, Digital Minister of Taiwan, has said "As Digital Minister, I have established a network of Participation Officers in each ministry. They serve as the links between the general public and the public sectors, and as channels for inter-agency collaboration" (Tang, no page number).

In contrast, I could say further that I don't see much transnationality, proper, in Taiwan politics at all, meaning that there are no foreigners in governmental positions here that I know of. Foreigners have spoken out in Taiwan quite a lot, their voices have been heard and their problems and needs have been addressed—but such solutions always come from *Taiwanese* politicians and legislators. And yet that is not quite true, for almost all Taiwanese politicians can speak English and other languages very well, and thus they have themselves entered into transnational spaces of interactivity and inter-communality (and I might point out Hugues Mignot, who served as Belgium's top representative to Taiwan from 1986 to 2006, and who spoke fluent Chinese and was a naturalized Taiwanese citizen, clearly making his newland home here—a transnational administrative worker closely allied with Taiwan's own government. Mignot died in May 2022). Further, Taiwan's active pursuits of relations with other countries internationally (that is, transnationally) bring the nation into a transnational world of bilateral collectivity, reciprocal treaty-making, mutual recognition, and lawmaking at the highest level. Needless to say, China enters the picture here, with its suppression of Taiwanese polities, and refusal to recognize the points just noted. This is definitely a negative, but it may just be that even China and Taiwan are participating in a certain transnational awareness, that is, they do "recognize" differences (and quite a few similarities) between themselves, and they have sought (very broadly) to settle these affairs, and in some senses, distinguish and concede to one another as sovereign states (there's that troublesome word and conception again). This may be stretching the point, but at some level Chinese and Taiwanese people see each other as rather different (but in turn, "the same") peoples in a given internationalized, transnational space, in which they have to interact in the ways described. This might be a unique take on the conception of what connective transnationalism can be, and I will return to this point in a discussion with students, below.

Further (and again), in terms of these conceptions, overtures, etc., Taiwan's recognition of its own native, indigenous peoples—each a "state" in some sense (in the same manner as Native Americans comprise their own tribal sovereignties)—can be seen as a true transnational move. Taiwan's embrace of foreign visitors of all kinds—whether traveling tourists or foreigners that choose to live here semi- or permanently (as this writer has)—also creates a true transnational, networked society. Approximately 550–800,000 foreigners live in Taiwan from countries all around the world (from taiwan.gov, Wikipedia, and other sources). Recently, the law in Taiwan was changed, allowing foreigners who meet certain requirements to take Taiwanese citizenship. While common in most other countries, this was next to impossible in Taiwan until this law was changed. Foreigners can now take Taiwanese citizenship, opening the nation into a globalized, transnational reality in its society (as we saw with Mignot, above). This sounds good, but only about 100 foreigners have been able to do this so far.

I have considered all of the above in my writing published in the *Taipei Times*, "New Approach to Diplomatic Bind," 8 October 2019. This study does not address transnationality specifically, but the ideas of statehood, governance, and recognition can be understood in these lights.

Taiwan has experienced many diplomatic quandaries, right up to recently, with the severance of diplomatic relations with Nicaragua in January 2022. Before that, as noted, the nation had severed ties with six other allies under President Tsai Ing-wen (蔡英文). Taiwan's (the Republic of China's) remaining 15 allies find themselves in a ticklish position, "supporting" a country (the ROC) that few other nations do, one which has largely been cast into the dustbin of history. This introduces the question of nationality (*transnationality* I want to say), and just what it can mean in world affairs today. To be sure, Taiwan's situation looks dire, and the question of its very "nationhood" appears to be at risk. In the end, Taiwan could be left with no diplomatic allies, a situation faced by a number of other "non-countries" in the world today. This is an uncomfortable reality to face—but perhaps not without a solution.

Taiwan as a nation has very little status in the world, and the Republic of China is doing no better. Yes, this seems odd in terms of the reality of the nation of Taiwan—a country with culture, history, peoples/ethnicities, languages, geography, world trade, laws, customs, norms, identity, and a functioning government. The simple reality is that Taiwan does function as just this in the international system, and few other countries would doubt this. Indeed, many another country has taken the ultimate step and "recognized" Taiwan/ROC as just this in the world (the United States comes that close, as do many others). But this does not alter the reality of Taiwan's diminishing role and connection in world affairs, the reduction of its "nationality" to very little.

I thus turn to a proposed answer, which I think could introduce a new transnational reality into the life and politics of Taiwan. On the one hand (there is more below), Taiwan might launch a new model of diplomatic concurrence, becoming a one-off, stand-alone entity that does not even need the recognition of others—it could still function as an independent transnation in the world. Quite frankly, I rather like this idea, and the introduction of an innovative new paradigm of international diplomacy could be a bold move by Taiwan, and introduce the very transnational (one might say "non-national") relations we are considering. This might evolve into something of the stateless world, populated by "world citizens" who have abandoned those often labored, synthetic attachments to home nations, an idea that has created endless conflict in the world, and in turn given rise to jingoistic, and populist/nationalist risings.[2] Such an idea might alter the very idea of the UN, and we may find ourselves modifying relations into a new *UM*, from the French *Union Mondiale*, Global Union.

In a word, my hope is that the above description can be seen in a positive light in Taiwan, and by the world at large, opening new pathways of transnationality, crossing borders and boundaries, introducing new conceptions of just what "nations" and "peoples" can be. This new approach may be called for in today's often-divided world. Taiwan and

[2] See how Horng-luen Wang writes, in a not-unpopular view that we have referred to, that "Nation-states may eventually decline, and in the future, there may exist a nation-less world where nationality and nationhood hold no significance at all" (111). I should probably add that later he reverses this view, writing "transnational flows of people, culture and capital during globalization may have ignored, subverted and devalued national boundaries and their associated states, but this does not necessarily imply the decline of nations and/or nation-states. By intensifying the interactions among different constituents of the global village, globalization may also assert and reinforce the institutional prerogatives of nations and nation-states, thereby re-emphasizing the significance—or even the necessity, as it were—of nationhood and nation-stateness" (111).

other nations may be faced with "going it alone" in the future, but maybe that is in fact a better outcome and will open doors onto new collaborative communicative experience. Let the transnational *UM* begin today!

Admittedly, I should probably step aside here and consider this idea, which is to ask, could such a global body be possible? At one level, it has been asked if such a "democratic" body (we assume it would be that) is possible at the international/transnational level. This possibility is called "cosmopolitan democracy" by David Held, a "democratic public law entrenched within and across borders…transcend[ing] the particular claims of nations and states and extend[ing] to all in the 'universal community'" (227–228). Such an approach "would allow representative democracy to function at a more than national level, whether regional or global" (Sørensen 123). This may or may not result in the "stateless world" I have proposed, but the idea seen in these lights appears viable. Samuel P. Huntington considered the possibilities of an "international system," which existed during the ages of colonialism and imperialism, when Europe ruled most of the world (and the same was true in prior imperial ages, including Sumerian, Greek, Hellenistic, Chinese, Indian, and Islamic), and for the most part it functioned reasonably effectually (nobody would excuse the realities that were taking place within the dominated countries of course). In contrast, Huntington writes, an "international society" exists when "states in an international system have 'common interests and common values,' 'conceive themselves to be bound by a common set of rules,' 'share in the working of common institutions,' and have 'a common culture or civilization'" (54).[3] This is probably going a bit far, but in fact we would argue that transnational travelers in newlands are working in these directions, if very broadly.

With all of the above, let's return to our central point: Taiwan, and its possible transnational character, which I have considered above in terms of governance, proper. I have argued for just this, and more, in "Taiwan is a true transnational state" in the *Taipei Times* on 3 July 2019. There I argued that Taiwan was a "transnational state in the true sense." I began my argument with a look at myself—a foreigner living in Taiwan, wherein I had been thrust into a new world of difference, a certain transnational "other" in this country. I have consistently been required to make certain alterations to my own worldview and perceptions of others during

[3] Quotes from Hedley Bull, *The Anarchical Society*, Columbia UP, 1977, pp. 9–13.

my (hopefully positive) interaction and collaboration with the Taiwanese people. In some senses, I am a bit less than "transnational" myself, as I have not mastered the Chinese language, and to be sure such efforts are essential in this new world, in order to construct and illumine new borders and spaces, better suited for understanding other peoples.

Broadly, in practice transnationalism refers to increased versatility and incorporation of processes that connect and define individuals, governments, and groups of all kinds (businesses, NGOs, NSAs, supranational organizations, educational groups, "emergent organizations," worker's cooperatives, community assemblies—all groups we have referred to thus far), such that they can mobilize effectively beyond state boundaries. Individuals, groups, institutions, and states are interacting with each other in a new global amplitude, where cultural and political characteristics are combined with evolving transnational engagements. To be sure, I have found myself in one such group, my Taiwanese friends and peers always eyeing me from the other side of the transnational fence.

Taiwan can most assuredly see itself in all of these lights, with many transnational/transitional actors having an impact here. Probably one key actor (though not that as such) are the social movements that have rocked Taiwan in recent years, with their efforts to redefine politics and culture. Such movements are in effect challenging the role of the state in national affairs and bringing citizens into the conversation. A look at Taiwan in these lights is truly enlightening: From the early democracy demonstrations, including the Wild Lily Movement (a 1990 student demonstration for democracy), the Wild Strawberry activists (a student protest in Taipei against Taiwan's Parade and Assembly Act), through the recent successes in LGBT rights, to the Sunflower protests. It has been a very active scene in Taiwan for many, many years. To be perfectly frank, these movements may not be "transnational" in the true sense—they are in the main composed of young Taiwanese citizens—but just as well, many people of other nationalities have assumed roles, indicating a blending of borders that is very much transnational (probably mostly seen in terms of international social networking and forums that worked in support of the movements). Most importantly, this indicates a new view onto what national/world affairs actually are and can be, and how such movements transgress the limits and norms of ordinary politics and (now seemingly hidebound) states. Such movements are in essence actors who are having an influence on how the state functions and makes decisions in a borderless environment. Taiwanese social movements have to be sure done all of this.

In related actions, many international groups and NGOs have slated forums, conferences, and demonstrations in Taiwan. Such moves are truly "transnational" in scope, with many countries and organizations participating in movements that truly do attempt to eliminate boundaries among people. And these are by no means the first such international assemblies that have occurred in Taiwan. In one important development, the Reporters Without Borders (*Reporters sans frontiers*) group established its first Asian bureau in Taipei in 2017. Also in 2017, the *Universiade* sports competition in Taipei indicated a transnational focus in the nation. These events, openings, and summits are yielding collective action locally, nationally, and internationally, and in turn forging links across national borders amid a new global civil society. In these ways, these transnational constructs are interconnected networks, with such systems promoting relationships and addressing common issues, despite geographical "limitations" (we can hardly call them that any more). Such is the "shrinking" of the global, and much less national, space in today's world.

References

Bevir, Mark, ed. "Transnational Governance." In *Encyclopedia of Governance*. Located at https://sk.sagepub.com/reference/governance/n546.xml.

Biedermann, Reinhard, 2017. "Taiwan's Polycentric Strategy Within the Environmental Regime Complex on Climate Change." *ASIEN 143* (April 2017), S. 25–46. Located at http://asienforschung.de/wp-content/uploads/2018/03/143_RA_Biedermann_ClimateChange_final.pdf.

Held, David, 1995. *Democracy and the Global Order: From the Modern State to Cosmopolitan Governance*. Stanford UP, © 1995 by David Held. Located at https://books.google.com.tw/books/about/Democracy_and_the_Global_Order.html?id=bkP4OVTlkjAC&redir_esc=y.

Hierlemann, Dominik, Stefan Roch, 2020. "Digital Participation in Taiwan: Takeaways for Europe." Published in *Participo*. Accessed 12 November, 2021 at https://medium.com/participo/digital-participation-in-taiwan-8f5b020afbc4#:~:text=Digital%20tools%20for%20citizens%E2%80%99%20participation%20have%20become%20a,Taiwan%20began%20its%20transition%20from%20authoritarianism%20towards%20democracy.

Huntington, Samuel P. 1996. *The Clash of Civilizations and the Remaking of World Order*. Simon and Schuster.

Pendery, David, 2019. "New Approach to Diplomatic Bind." *Taipei Times*, 6 October 2019. Located at http://www.taipeitimes.com/News/editorials/archives/2019/10/06/2003723453.

———. 2019. "Taiwan Is a True Transnational State." *Taipei Times*, 3 July 2019. Located at https://www.taipeitimes.com/News/editorials/archives/2019/07/03/2003718013.

Sørensen, Ninna Nyberg 2007. *Living Across Worlds: Diaspora, Development and Transnational Engagement*. International Organization for Migration.

Taipei Times, staff writer. "Former Belgium, Luxembourg Envoy Dies at Age 80," 2 May 2022.

Taiwan.gov.tw. Located at https://www.taiwan.gov.tw.

Tang, Audrey, 2019. "Inside Taiwan's New Digital Democracy." *The Economist*. Accessed 21 February 2022 at https://www.economist.com/open-future/2019/03/12/inside-taiwans-new-digital-democracy.

Wang, Horng-luen, 2000. "National Reflections on National Imaginations in Taiwan." *Theory, Culture and Society*, 17.4: 93–117. Accessed 3 March, 2022 at https://www.ios.sinica.edu.tw/people/personal/hlwang/hlwang2000-1.pdf.

Wikipedia. "Demographics of Taiwan." Located at https://en.wikipedia.org/wiki/Demographics_of_Taiwan.

———. "Trans-Pacific Partnership." Located at https://en.wikipedia.org/wiki/Trans-Pacific_Partnership.

———. "List of Political Parties in Taiwan." Located at https://en.wikipedia.org/wiki/List_of_political_parties_in_Taiwan.

CHAPTER 9

Transnational Migration

Abstract Immigration is seen as key driver of transnational identity and subjectivity. "Social Fields" within transnationalism are viewed. Homelands and newlands are introduced. People in homelands communicating with transnational migrants and the constant flow of economic and social remittances. A new transnational *Weltanschauung*, perspective and position. Huntington's "population movements are the motor of history" is cited, and antagonism to immigration. IOM estimates of immigration worldwide, international migrants as a driver of transnationalism. Political transnational activities and international migration activities are reviewed. Migration within broader geopolitical and global dynamics, linked to economics and globalization is looked at. Transnationalism and politics, society, economics, education, and individuality, with processes that cross borders and inculcate new relations among individuals and groups, outside of traditional state boundaries.

Keywords Immigration · Social fields · Homelands · Newlands · Remittances · *Weltanschauung* · Motor of history · Huntington · Political activities

To return to the basics, as noted, immigration has been a key driver of transnational experience, behavior, and subjectivity. Simply put, and

D. Pendery, *Transnational Taiwan*,
https://doi.org/10.1007/978-981-19-4368-3_9

no doubt as we have seen, "The movement of people brings the movement of new ideas, religions, beliefs, etc. in its wake" (Held, et al., 285), and "notions of citizenship and national identity are being renegotiated in response to contemporary patters of global migration" (Held, et al. 326). Said notes that today's world (and the imperial/colonial words that preceded it) has produced "more refugees, migrants, displaced persons, exiles, homeless wanderers, nomads, vagrants than ever before in history," (reworded from 332). The struggles of these peoples have produced new boundaries, new transnations connected with original nations. These conditions "articulate the tensions, irresolutions, and contradictions in the overlapping territories," now home to the new transnationals (from Said 332). This has all led to worlds "between languages," with the release of "unhoused, decentered, and exilic energies, energies whose incarnation today is the migrant" (Said 332).

The map from Held et al. below (298) shows the major routes of migration in the modern world. We can see that migration has occurred in virtually all areas of the globe as people have sought to redefine their lives in transnational contexts (Map 9.1). The above immigrants engage in transnational activities, creating "social fields"[1] that connect their home country with their new country of residence ("homelands" and "newlands"). Further, migration experiences "[take] place within transnational social space," and go beyond "those who actually migrate to those who do not necessarily move but are connected to migrants through networks of social relations they sustain across borders" (Sørensen 7). The people in the homelands communicating with the transnational migrants "are exposed to a constant flow of economic and social remittances on a regular basis, which might change their identities, world views and aspirations" (Sørensen 7–8). This is to say that "incorporation into a new state and enduring attachments to the countries of origin are not necessarily binary opposites" (Sørensen 8). So, a "cross-border" strengthening of not just ties, but veritable character and identification, a newfound *Weltanschauung*, perspective and position, are in effect, impacting all parties in the transnational world. No doubt we see this in Taiwan with its populations of peoples from all around the world deciding to

[1] Linkages, perhaps primarily in terms of social networking, but also simply by way of communicative association and endeavor with other peoples, which create economic, political, and socio-cultural contacts.

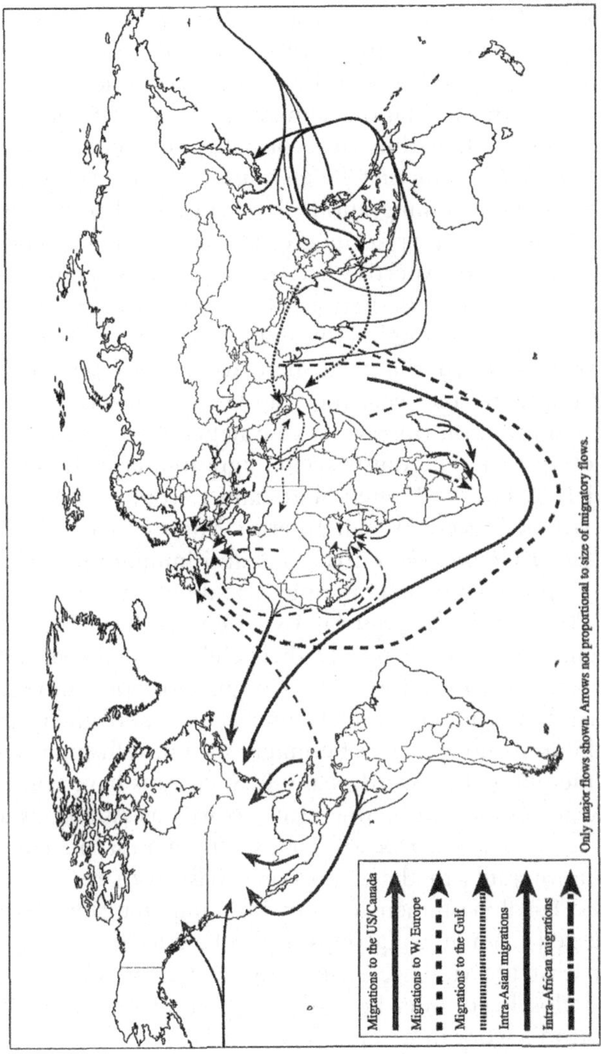

Map. 9.1 Major global migrations, 1945–1995

educate themselves, work and live here. To be sure, I have witnessed and experienced just this in my two decades in Taiwan.

In terms of immigration, Samuel P. Huntington noted that "population movements are the motor of history" (*The Clash of Civilizations* 198), a view we would not disagree with. Modernization (of culture, national ethos, industry and manufacturing, commerce, trade and professionalism, world view, transportation, and technology) have led to this point, and migration itself, within this constellation, "becomes a self-reinforcing process" (*The Clash of Civilizations* 199). Huntington goes on, later in his book, that "immigration…[is] a potential source of new vigor and human capital," with "priority given to able, qualified, energetic people with the talents and expertise needed by the host country" and that "new migrants and their children [are] assimilated into the culture of the country…" (304). Though Huntington will in the end take a thoroughly negative view on this take, here we can see the reality of immigration and migrants, and what they can bring to newlands.

As just noted, Huntington observes a true negative in terms of all we are discussing, noting that antagonism to immigration reached new highs in the 1980s and 1990s in the United States and Europe—"Immigration must be totally stopped" said French Interior Minister Charles Pasqua in 1993 (*The Clash of Civilizations* 201), and anti-immigration measures in California were prominent at that time (seemingly a welcome zone for immigrants, California's Proposition 187, denying health, education and welfare benefits to illegal aliens and their children in 1994 certainly showed otherwise). In 1995, the U.S. Commission on Immigration Reform recommended reducing annual immigration, and giving preference to certain children and spouses of immigrants, but refusing privileges for other family members. In a word, many U.S. citizens have considered the arrival of Mexicans and Latin Americans, as well as Asians, as a true threat, while in Europe the arrival of Turkish immigrants in Germany, and of Muslim immigrants in the Euro zone, has given rise to heated reprisals. We need hardly comment on just how much anti-immigration rhetoric has emerged from angry groups in the United States, up to the present day, not least the violence against Asians that was seen in early 2022. We should closely consider how this continues to be true. We will examine Huntington's work in greater detail below.

The IOM estimates that one in 30 persons worldwide are migrants. Current estimates say that there were around 281 million international migrants in the world in 2020. The estimated number of international migrants has increased over the past five decades. "Understanding changes in scale, emerging trends and shifting demographics related to global social and economic transformations, such as migration, help us make sense of the changing world we live in and plan for the future," says the IOM.

The integration of international migrants seeking new economic and demographic futures in developed countries is a driver of transnationalism. Beyond just filling a demand for low-wage workers, migration fills demographic gaps created by declining and aging populations. This is true in most industrialized and westernized nations, which although not always thought of as sending our waves of migrants into newlands, have no doubt had a significant impact on all that we are examining (the United States has an estimated nine million emigrants out of the country, most, interestingly enough, in Mexico [from Wikipedia, "Emigration from the United States"]). In reverse, today, migration accounts for most population growth in western countries.

Political transnational activities can range from retained membership in political parties in one's country of origin, to participating in political activities and social movements in the newland, to writing editorials in one or the other, or simply lobbying a local (native) elected official. As we have looked at, actual adoption of newland citizenship may often come into play, and could lead to migrants being elected to office.[2] No doubt they would still retain connection to their homelands, and such association would come into play in policymaking in the newland.

Simply put, migration is very likely the most important driver of all that we have looked at. Transnationalism has significant implications for the way we conceptualize immigration. Traditionally, immigration has been seen as an autonomous process, driven by conditions such as poverty and overpopulation in the country of origin and unrelated to conditions such as foreign policy and generalized social policy in the receiving country. Even though overpopulation, economic stagnation, and poverty

[2] Readers are probably aware that Taiwanese-American Michelle Wu was elected Boston's first female mayor in 2021, a true transnational development. Other Taiwanese have been elected in other states as well. Wu is usually called a "Taiwanese-American," and although Bourne voiced some objections to such hyphenation earlier, it is just such peoples who have long carried the transnational torch in America.

all continue to create pressures for migrants, such problems alone are not enough to produce (or reduce) international migration flows. There are many countries, for example, which lack significant emigration history despite longstanding poverty. Also, most international immigration flows from the global South to the global North are not made up of the poorest of the poor, but, often, by professionals and working-class men and women. In addition, there are countries with high levels of job creation that continue to witness emigration on a large scale.

As seen above, migration will always stem from broader geopolitical and global dynamics, and the transnationalism that emerges from this will probably continue to be linked to economics and globalization. For some, the discussion ends here, and it cannot be denied that there are systematic structural relations linking globalization, economies, and migration/immigration/emigration (we might again call this liberalized, capitalism-based transnationalism). In any case, the emergence of a global economy, with all of the migration that goes along with this, has led to these views, and created economic, cultural, and ideological links between industrialized and developing countries. We will look at this in more detail in "Transnational Business and Work" below.

Transnationalism as concept, theory, and experience has led to important considerations in politics, society, economics, education, and individuality. In practice, transnational immigration refers to increasing functional integration of processes that cross borders and inculcate new relations among individuals and groups, outside of traditional state boundaries. All citizens are interacting in a new "global space," wherein cultural and political qualities of varied societies are being combined with emerging multi/transnational characteristics.

References

Held, David, Anthony McGrew, David Goldblatt, Jonathan Perraton, 1999. *Global Transformations: Politics, Economics, and Culture*. Polity Press.

Huntington, Samuel P. 1996. *The Clash of Civilizations and the Remaking of World Order*. Simon and Schuster.

International Organization for Migration, UN Migration. "Resettlement," at https://medialib.iom.int/galleries/browse/resettlement?content=any.

Said, Edward W., 1993–1994. *Culture and Imperialism*. Vintage Books.

Sørensen, Ninna Nyberg 2007. *Living Across Worlds: Diaspora, Development and Transnational Engagement*. International Organization for Migration.

Wikipedia, “Emigration from the United Sates.” Located at https://en.wikipedia.org/wiki/Emigration_from_the_United_States.
———, “Population Growth.” Located at https://en.wikipedia.org/wiki/Population_growth.
———, “Transnationalism.” Located at https://en.wikipedia.org/wiki/Transnationalism.

CHAPTER 10

Transnational Business and Work

Abstract Businesspersons, entrepreneurs, technicians and migrant workers are traveling worldwide and bringing new experience into their work relations, crafting transnational strategies and working on joint activities with a transnational focus. Transnational business, it will be seen, has advantages and disadvantages, is decentralized, localized. A transnational capitalist class and global working class of migrants is emerging. Expansion of transnational business in order to compete globally will be seen. Local operations of international businesses is a new norm. Monetary remittances to homelands are now extensive, larger than international economic aid to developing countries. Numbers of Taiwanese working overseas fluctuates but has grown. Transnational capitalism and globalization are further looked at. Taiwan has developed local science parks, increasing transnationalism, and impacting education and immigration. Taiwan admits large numbers of international immigrants, working in Taiwan. New transnational business activities are creating the emergence of highly mobile groups of entrepreneurs, executives and specialists.

Keywords Transnational business · Work · Migrants · Guest workers · Transnational business strategies · Localization · Overseas students · Monetary remittances · Taiwanese working abroad

D. Pendery, *Transnational Taiwan*,
https://doi.org/10.1007/978-981-19-4368-3_10

We have seen many instances of transnational business and workers already in our analysis, and seen how businesspersons, entrepreneurs, technicians, and migrant workers are traveling worldwide and bringing new life and experience into their work relations, crafting transnational (some would simply say "international") strategies and working on joint activities with a transnational focus. While the advantages to such professional activity may seem obvious—increased competences without major outlays, greater business flexibility, knowledge sharing, competitive advantage and increased specialization, accelerated learning processes, reduced costs for joint development of products and services—the disadvantages must also be considered—reduction in strategic autonomy of companies, the challenges of structural, systemic, and cultural coordination, and the difficulty of combining varied, multicultural objectives and interests (European Commission). Transnational business may generally become decentralized, with bases in various countries, extending their operations in order to implement higher levels of local responsiveness. In contrast, traditional multinational corporations are principally national(ized) companies, simply with foreign subsidiaries. A transnational corporation may not consider any particular country its corporate home base, and they are thus able to maintain a greater degree of responsiveness to local markets.

In terms of political economy, a new and growing transnational capitalist class is having ever more influence in countries near and far, native and adopted. This has led to the growth of corporate networks, a "global working class" of migrants, and the transnationalization (in the broad senses looked at so far) of policymaking and elite systems within globally connected MNCs. These transnational businesses engage in value-creating activities across national borders, which to be sure indicates exactly what they encounter in their operations. "Faced with accelerated globalization, managers often make decisions to expand a firm's transnationality in order to enable the firm to effectively compete with rivals on a global scale" (Wikipedia, "Transnational corporation"). They will employ senior executives, marketing personnel, and technicians from many countries and attempt to make decisions from a transnational/global perspective, as opposed to one centralized and/or nationalized headquarters. Such transnational actions may create better relationships between nations.

Held et al. note that immigrants into newlands generally "fill the bottom rungs of the labour market," but there is more at work (324).

In fact, "In many OECD [Organisation for Economic Co-operation and Development] countries a significant percentage of foreign workers are highly skilled professionals" (324). These authors note that immigrants in both the higher- and lower-skilled niches of labor markets have expanded in recent years. Even in the United States, the demand for home workers and domestics (generally lower-paid) has increased, while "the expansion of high-tech and service industries has created jobs in professional, managerial and technical occupations—often filled by migratory transnationals. As well, "Immigrant communities have also been significant in creating jobs and businesses themselves" (325). In the UK, "Asian entrepreneurs have revitalized the retail, catering, textile and clothing industries," and this is also true in Germany, France, and the United States. The online *Smartling,* writes how companies that have extensive operations in Taiwan have implemented transnational strategies. McDonald's has adapted to the local market, using, warm wood colors, earthy tones, and graphic art pieces on the walls. Long-order counters have been replaced with checkout counters and self-order kiosks, and the company now uses a very convenient order/pick-up design system. The company introduced rice burgers in Taiwan, but these were less successful. Unilever embodied a classic approach of "thinking globally, acting locally," hiring local Taiwanese managers to run in-country operations. Nike has adopted social media tactics (certainly popular in Taiwan). Samsung, the Korean electronics company, uses Chinese skillfully in its marketing (I have noted many Western companies doing just this), and Coca-Cola (可口可樂, kěkǒukělè in Taiwan) has subtly adapted its messaging to cater to local markets in Taiwan, designing bottles that feature attractions across Taiwan (above from *Taiwan News, Smartling,* Liao, and Yi-chih Wang).

In light of the above, we can see that transnational economic activities are deep and wide. Business investments across borders, and monetary remittances to homelands are extensive (estimated at $717 billion by the IOM). Such economic connections have linked (trans)nations in entirely new ways, with monetary returns to homelands now greater than actual international aid provided to developing countries, and economic connections by way of newly opened business investments creating wide-ranging new connectivity and economic growth (this is particularly true in Taiwan and China, with, as noted, many Taiwanese businesspersons living and working in China today). This flood of shared resources may mean that for some nations, development prospects are inextricably linked—if not dependent upon—the economic activities of their respective migrant populations or diasporas.

501,000 Taiwanese worked overseas in 2020, though this number has dropped (from *FocusTaiwan*). And as well, consider the vast range of businesses in Taiwan, and their international markets and associates, in fields of technology, banking, bicycles, precision industry, airlines, shipbuilding, mobile telecommunications, aerospace, biotechnology, agriculture, health and medical, and more. In the end, Taiwan's embeddedness in globalization has "facilitated the penetration and circulation of transnational flows of commodities, people, capital and symbolic goods" (Horng-luen Wang 105). We have considered the entire conception of globalization and its economic aspects above, and in some senses backed away from this view, but that does not diminish its importance in our conversation. In a word, the views of many on migrant workers, MNCs, and global money flow are all, as noted, pegged to profitability, and we wish to explore beyond these bounds. Many have argued that transnational capitalism has occurred by way of little more than the monopolization and centralization of capital by powerful players. These critics hope for, rather than a "transnationalism from above"—doings organized by powerful institutional actors, MNCs and the like—a "transnationalism from below," that is, an expression of popular resistance, and grassroots activities that will connect workers, cooperatives, and popular social and political movements, all affecting "power relations, cultural constructions, economic interactions, and, more generally, social organization at the level of the locality" (Smith 6). This would all remove the conceptions we are examining from strictly economic views, and take them into a more sociocultural analysis.

In Taiwan, the creation of the Hsinchu Science-based Industrial Park in 1980 was a key development, attracting foreign migrant workers (many high-level professionals and technicians), as well as the return of educated Taiwanese to Taiwan. The result has been "a critical mass of creative, Western-educated people that attracted more returnees" (O'Neil, no page number), with Taiwanese emigrants, having studied and worked overseas, bringing home knowledge, business connections, and a greater international awareness and expertise, which they have provided to the government and the private sector through informal and formal networks—a beneficial circle. Taiwan has at least two other such science/industrial parks, including the Central Taiwan Science Park in Taichung, and Southern Taiwan Science Park in Tainan, and to be sure these enterprises encompass the entirety of the technology industry in Taiwan, not least it's world-class semi-conductor industries, which are to be sure transnational businesses *par excellence*.

In sum, Taiwan is no doubt a key regional player in this economic transnational life, not least by way of its admission of countless migrant workers across its own borders. Such workers—many construction workers, a handful of more technical personnel, a few teachers and perhaps translators, and a large group of "home workers" (almost all female), who take care of elderly Taiwanese—are somewhat common here, with the generally booming economy attracting many such employees. Conditions have been reasonably good, though there has been some call for improvement, and it has been observed that in fact conditions are not ideal in Taiwan for these peoples, and greater attention needs to be paid to providing them with rights and other necessities for living, reducing discrimination, allowing longer-term work stays, and improving salaries. It is hoped that these will all become realities in the near future (see "Taiwan should lead on migrant rights," unsigned editorial, *Taipei Times*, 26 March, 2022). There have been occasional cases of abuse, occasional conflict and violence, but for the most part, it has not been a serious problem. We will see this issue again in our look at "Transnational Conflict, Security, and Militarization," below.

Related to all of the above is the use of various languages in business operations, which we have considered thus far, and will look at again below when we see the prominence of such study in Taiwan.

We have seen in the modern transnational world the need for migrant workers (often called "guest workers, *gastarbeiter* in German), contract workers, and varied technicians, who make moves from less-developed to more developed/industrialized (often booming) economies (to be sure Taiwan has a place in this reality), and the related "significance of transnational business activities, causing the emergence of highly mobile groups of entrepreneurs, executives and specialists" (Yeoh 17–18). As well, the development of a globalized world economic network has resulted in "cross-border flows of all sorts and…the formation of transnational networks in the economic, cultural, political and social spheres"—not least in Asia (Yeoh 21). In a word, in all of this, we see the value of the "local-transnational" realities and circuitries of migrant workers in and out of Taiwan.

References

Focus Taiwan, 16 December 2021. "Number of Taiwanese Working Overseas in 2020 Hits 11-Year Low." Located at https://focustaiwan.tw/business/202112160016.

Held, David, Anthony McGrew, David Goldblatt, Jonathan Perraton, 1999. *Global Transformations: Politics, Economics, and Culture*. Polity Press

Liao, George, *Taiwan News*. 2020. "Coca-Cola Launches four Taiwan-Themed Bottles." Located at https://www.taiwannews.com.tw/en/news/3949580.

O'Neil, Kevin, 2003. "Brain Drain and Gain: The Case of Taiwan." Migration Policy Institute. Accessed 2 March 2022 at https://www.migrationpolicy.org/article/brain-drain-and-gain-case-taiwan.

Smith, Michael Peter; Eduardo Guarnizo, eds., 1998. *Transnationalism From Below, Comparative Urban and Community Research V6*, Transaction Publishers. Accessed 25 December, 2021 at https://books.google.com.tw/books/about/Transnationalism_from_Below.html?id=zTxYLmr7g_YC&redir_esc=y.

Taipei Times, unsigned editorial, 26 March, 2022. "Taiwan Should Lead on Migrant Rights." Located at https://taipeitimes.com/News/editorials/archives/2022/03/26/2003775463.

Taiwan News, staff reporter, 2005. "McDonald's Offering Rice Burgers." Located at https://www.taiwannews.com.tw/en/news/135948.

Wang, Horng-luen, 2000. "National Reflections on National Imaginations in Taiwan." *Theory, Culture and Society.* Volume: 17 Issue: 4, 93–117. Accessed 3 March, 2022 at https://www.ios.sinica.edu.tw/people/personal/hlwang/hlwang2000-1.pdf.

Wang, Yi-chih, *CommonWealth Magazine*, 2020. "Taiwan's McDonald's 2.0 Moving Fast-Food Upmarket." Located at https://english.cw.com.tw/article/article.action?id=2768.

Wikipedia, "Transnational Corporation." Located at https://en.wikipedia.org/wiki/Transnational_corporation.

Yeoh, Brenda S.A., Katie Willis. 2004. *State/Nation/Transnation: Perspectives on Transnationalism in the Asia-Pacific*. Routledge.

CHAPTER 11

Transnational Subjectivity

Abstract Community, political and commonwealth identity and subjectivity are examined, along with Taiwanese travels and development of new identity. Expatriates, and development of new subjectivity, jobs, homes, marriages, children. New openness of experience and place, and relation to homelands. Dual and multiple national loyalties. Activities, sets of relations, new social fields are viewed. Taiwanese in Taiwan are seen without transnational lives, a statist view of life, but interacting with foreigners here, engaging in international affairs, speaking other languages. Taiwan pursuit of sovereignty, unique identity and independence. "Unofficial" and non-state activities as transnational. Transnational psychology of new rootless migrants. Multiple simultaneous histories.

Keywords Subjectify · Identity · Newlands · Homelands · Multiple loyalties · Social fiends · Statist view · Foreign language · Sovereignty · Independence · Unofficial relations · Transnational psychology · Multiple simultaneous histories

In terms of all of the above, the communities and polities and commonwealths they comprise, we might ask, "What really is the transnational

D. Pendery, *Transnational Taiwan*,
https://doi.org/10.1007/978-981-19-4368-3_11

subjectivity of these peoples?"[1] That is, who and what sorts of people are they, and why do they engage in the travels and relocations that they do? What are their hopes and dreams, their daily experiences, their aims and desires, their struggles and problems, their worldviews, the very ways they transact and interact with others in homelands and newlands? How do they live their lives as "transnationals" in globalized contexts in our world today? How do the scores of migrants, refugees, exiles, tourists, overseas students, elites, immigrants, travelers, expatriates, aliens, evacuees, and nomads engage in their large-scale movements and interactivity, their communicative endeavors, their correspondence and expression, within this networked world? Let's take a look at this (and needless to say I am focusing on the Taiwanese people, and even now I recall the stories of Judy Chen and Ciloue Cheng Stewart, examined above).

In the present day, "Taiwan's population is traveling across national boundaries regularly and frequently" (Horng-luen Wang 95), and given this, "we may continue to see a transnational effect on [their] identity" (Horng-luen Wang 101). Taiwanese people now "interact with people from other parts of the world more intensely," and thus, "citizenship and nationality are becoming more and more problematized" (Horng-luen Wang 96). Wang writes of the incorporation of "elements of 'internationalization/globalization' into the new Taiwanese identity" (Horng-luen Wang 99), and to be sure, we can see here the essential elements of transnational subjectivity at play, and recognize that this is as true with Taiwanese as with any people in the world. In the end, streams of Taiwanese people traveling, working, studying, and living abroad have given rise to the fact that "transnational experiences have had a profound impact upon identity formation and transformation for the people in Taiwan" (Horng-luen Wang 109). In a word, the very mobility of Taiwanese people traveling and settling abroad has given rise to a new world view. Hsu stresses that the geographical dispersal and mobility of the Taiwanese enables them to see a new world of, in essence, transnational players, and these people are in turn playing an increasingly important role on the global stage (from Horng-luen Wang 98). I discuss Taiwanese people here, but I could just as easily turn it about, and consider the foreign transnationals living in Taiwan.

[1] Note, I could just as well say "identity" here and following.

At the highest level, we can see insight into these factors, features, and fluctuations in all we have examined thus far. Thus, we find these are a transactive, collaborationist, creative people very much *involved in, ramified with, entangled within,* and *living in,* their newlands, with connections of course to their homelands—the varied places in which they subsist, persist, and exist. They are a governed people, very much in touch with all that is governmental—that which controls, administers, accounts, oversees, designates, directs, authorizes, socializes, attends to…the list goes on and on in terms of just how people are *controlled,* but at the same with a given *uncontrolledness* (call it simply, freedom), in terms of all that is administrative, bureaucratic, legal, legislative, and national; but as well social, civil, mutual, communal, and local.

And so, to the central question: Who are these peoples who seem to so much enjoy living in newlands, ensconced in unique cultures, living in extraordinary new places, surrounded and challenged by unfamiliar languages, interacting with dissimilar people, working in neoteric jobs, marrying foreign partners, and embracing unusual values, issues, and worldviews that are, as often as not, very, very different from what they have experienced before? In a word, we view profound, newfound affiliations and new senses of belonging in transnational spaces. This might simply be seen as the world of the expatriate, which readers of this volume know I am one with (20 years in Taiwan, indeed!). Expatriates certainly experience all of what we see here, but there is more to it than simply being "outside" in a newland (though being an "other" in life is still very important). "Are we all transnationals now?" asks one analyst, and although this might be going a bit far, we might view all of these ideas, issues, influences, and features in terms of our "native++" subjectivities/identities (Dahinden, no page number).

What is found in transnational subjectivity is a "future politics of openness and plurality" (very much seen in terms of "governance," as above) (Dobson 1), and such a subjectivity is formed in the "imagining of [identities that have] taken on a transnational dimension, even though their bodies are still confined to, or hiding within, the national space" (Sun 55). In other words, transnational subjectivity may be formed in the "liminal space between the homeland and host land…" (this view is also seen as a sort of "deterritorialization" in this work) (Sun 55–56).

Sun writes that "transnational subjectivity can not only be articulated discursively, but also performed bodily" (195) and it is both "partial and plural" (103). There is a "complex contour of transnational imagination…fraught with tension and ambiguity" (195). The more difficult and sometimes terrifying elements of the diasporic narrative "create powerful ideas of homeland that seem more deeply territorial than ever" (Appadurai in Sun 115; and this seems to contest the notion of "deterritorialization seen above). "[T]he experience of movement from, and shuttling back to, the home(land) makes 'travel' a legitimate metaphor for the formation of migrant subjectivity" (Sun 87). We see a "liminal, slip-zone" in transnationality, which becomes an "unpredictable place and manifests itself in unexpected time" (Sun 55). All of this can be connected to ideas of extensive Taiwan travel, looked at above.

Transnationalism may refer to "people who have dual or multiple national loyalties, all of which may be primary" (Dunn 17), who indulge in specific *activities* (maintaining, constructing, and strengthening linkages with their homelands and newlands, and including acts such as remittances, gifts, correspondence, property ownership, political activities, and various forms of emotional networking); *sets of relations* (between migrants functioning in civil societies in homelands and newlands); *new social fields* or *contexts* (deterritorialization, ideas of homeland and newland, "spaces" as living environments); and *perspective* (world citizen, alien, traveler, migrant, expatriate and the very idea of a *Weltanschauung*) (from Dunn, 17). In sum, we witness the "multiple ties and interactions linking people or institutions across the borders of nation-states"—a simple enough definition of transnationality, proper (Vertovec in Dunn 16). And again, all of this can be connected to ideas of extensive Taiwan travel.

The above inclines me to comment on an overall view of the Taiwanese people. This is to say that the people I am referring to are, in the main, not true transnationals, those living abroad, which I have most often referred to, but are in fact simply Taiwanese people living in Taiwan. Thus, throughout much of their experience they have had a relatively "statist" view onto life, communication and interconnections, not least in terms of Taiwan's diplomatic presence and non-presence in world affairs. This is a key point, as diplomacy in general, and perhaps Taiwan's particularly—troubled presence as it is in the world—has long revolved around questions of sovereignty, presence, recognition, autonomy, self-government, the value of statist democracy, freedom, and often, independence. These questions and problems almost always revolve around the state proper, as for example in Taiwan's efforts to be involved in the UN.

While all of this is true, a solely statist, technocratic, collectivist, centralist, corporatist, doctrinaire look is not enough. There is much more going on in Taiwan, and at one high level, Taiwanese people remain transnational in their very connections with all the entities that enter into play in these discussions, not least transnational groupings like the EU, NGOs of all stripes, NSAs, various transnational social movements, the UN itself, and, simply, all of the nations that do indeed interact with Taiwan, whether as diplomatically recognized presences (or lack thereof), or the plethora of "institutes," "offices," "trade centers," and "associations" from other countries that make their presence known in Taiwan.[2] In a word, Taiwan does indeed have "relations" with any number of countries and other organizations all around the world, and that most of these relations are "unofficial" makes them yet more transnational, and free of the statist baggage that diplomatic formalities introduce. In a word, "Taiwan provides compelling evidence for the need to reconceptualize the relationship between [nation states proper, international institutions, the essence of globalization] and the nation/nation-state" (additional wording in Horng-luen Wang 112). We can also consider the Taiwanese people, proper, and see that they have fairly wide worldviews (the response to the Russian invasion in Ukraine was very widespread, and upwards of NT$300 million was raised within five days to support the Ukrainian people, with connections made through Poland to distribute the money; a government-designated account also raised money for the effort; and President Tsai Ing-wen and other officials announced they would donate one month's salary to aid humanitarian relief efforts [from *Yahoo News*, *Reuters*]). Consider all this and recall how Sun stated that subjectivities are taking on transnational aspects, even though many people are still living in their homelands, their national spaces.

Interestingly enough, a "transnational psychology" conception has developed in response to an ever-more interconnected world, and the varied emotional phenomena and reactions that transcend nation-state

[2] Note that Horng-luen Wang writes that "the increasing importance of international organizations and transnational institutions [within the parameters of Taiwan's diplomatic and to some extent social efforts] has given Taiwanese people stronger aspirations to pursue a recognized nationhood or nation-stateness, as Taiwan's exclusion from these organizations and institutions in global communities has fostered a sense of injustice and collective anxiety" (with additional wording, page 110). This is a worthy point to consider, and points toward my own analyses of the state-ness of Taiwan, and how this has interrupted, to some extent, actual transnational flows and feelings.

boundaries (even Wikipedia has a "Transnational psychology" page). Going back, the prior impact of colonization and imperialism have left many peoples in some sense "rootless," "stateless," unsure of exactly where they stand, and in essence connected (or unconnected) in varied ways in "other" places. Globalization can be seen similarly, having left many "have nots" out of seemingly increasingly rich and prosperous nation's economic states. Psychologists are working with and treating inhabitants in newlands, and introducing new methods in local communities to examine the psychological challenges faced by these people, outside typical nation-state boundaries and borders. In one respect, this branch of psychology opens up new frontiers that take into consideration new swathes of people from many different populaces and areas around the world.

Further, socio-cultural transnational reflections include analysis of migrant and marginal populations who are experiencing "multiple simultaneous histories," in which transnational (and to some extent national) activities cover a disparate range of social and cultural transactions, through which significance, ideas, and sensibilities are exchanged among peoples—what is called the exchange of "social remittances"—which provide unique forms of social capital, networking, and relationships between migrants and their homeland connections. This is taking place not least through exchanges on the Internet, with all that can entail. All of this introduces challenges in terms of exactly how migrants relate and act within their newlands, while keeping connected to their home countries. It is said that migrant's lives are always rooted in a particular place and time, in addition to any changes they have enacted.

Take all these points into consideration, and as well, I have referred to the fact that almost all Taiwanese politicians speak other languages, and that language study is very prominent in Taiwanese education. As well, Taiwanese high-school graduates studying abroad rose 20% in 2019 (*Taiwan News*), and as many as 75,000 Taiwanese students were studying abroad in 2019–2020 (mostly in the United States, Australia, Japan, and Canada [from *Statista*]). Consider the thousands and thousands of foreigners living, working, and studying in Taiwan right now, and you begin to see a transnational overlay throughout Taiwanese society, extending not only from the actual migration of Taiwanese people around the world, to the times that the people in the nation interact with other countries, seeking recognition and other such diplomatic details, to the lives of politicians, businesspeople, workers, and students, very much connected by way of language around the world. And finally, the essential *Weltanschauung* of a challenged nation seeks to connect and interact with others, to find an accepted place in the global/transnational environment, and one that very much sympathizes with other nations with serious (and sometimes similar) problems.

As noted above, the people I call "Taiwanese" are as often as not, simply that, and not truly "transnational" in all of the ways described in this work. That is to say, the Taiwanese that I know are living in Taiwan, and are not living in new places and cultures as described throughout this work. This may be different from the aboriginal Taiwanese considered, who although are in essence in the same such "living in" space in Taiwan, do have the traveling and intercontinental experiences of their descendants stirring in their ancestral memories. Of course, there are any number of Taiwanese people who do indeed live in foreign countries and are indeed living in transnational spaces, and also all the travelers out of Taiwan visiting new lands, and as well simply the Taiwanese living in Taiwan who are in effect displaying transnational qualities and characters, speaking other languages, etc.

I here conclude my look at, principally, Taiwanese transnational subjectivity. I hope this analysis and these views have provided an interpretation of the life, experiences, engagement, consciousness/conscientiousness, attitudes, affections, being and character of what I am terming in the broadest senses, a "true transnational people."

In conclusion, the rising of the conception of a genuine "Taiwanese Identity," and the independence that this suggests, has been a very important issue in Taiwan for some time now. This has given rise to an attachment to the nation of Taiwan that has become extreme in many instances. And such an attachment to "nation" does indeed reduce and/or eliminate any feelings of transnational identity. And so, this is a new-ish reality in Taiwan, which may detract from, but not wholly abnegate, our main focus.

References

Dahinden, Janine, 2009. "Are We All Transnationals Now? Network Transnationalism and Transnational Subjectivity: The Differing Impacts of Globalization on the Inhabitants of a Small Swiss City." *Ethnic and Racial Studies*, 32.8, 1365–1386. Accessed 7 February, 2022 at https://www.tandfonline.com/doi/abs/10.1080/01419870802506534?journalCode=rers20.

Dobson, Kit. Date unknown. "Transnational Subjectivities: Roy Miki's Surrender and Global Displacements." Accessed 17 February, 2022 at https://journals.lib.unb.ca/index.php/scl/article/view/10572/11158.

Dunn, Kevin M., 2005. "A Paradigm of Transnationalism for Migration Studies." *New Zealand Population Review*, 31.2, 15–31. © 2005 Population Association of New Zealand. Accessed 15 March, 2022 at https://www.westernsydney.edu.au/__data/assets/pdf_file/0020/26633/A26.pdf.

Focus Taiwan 16 December 2021. "Number of Taiwanese Working Overseas in 2020 Hits 11-Year Low." Located at https://focustaiwan.tw/business/202112160016.

Reuters 2 March, 2022. "Taiwan President to Donate a Month's Salary for Ukraine Relief Efforts." Located at https://www.reuters.com/world/china/taiwan-president-donate-salary-ukraine-relief-efforts-2022-03-02/.

Statista. "Number of Students from Taiwan Studying Abroad in Academic Year 2019/20, by Major Destination Countries." Located at https://www.statista.com/statistics/1092368/taiwan-students-studying-abroad-by-destination-country/.

Sun, Wanning, 2002. *Leaving China: Media, Migration, and Transnational Imagination*. Rowman and Littlefield Publishers. Accessed 15 March, 2022 at https://books.google.com.tw/books/about/Leaving_China.html?id=xLmvgTnTYHwC&redir_esc=y.

Wang, Horng-luen, 2000. 'National Reflections on National Imaginations in Taiwan." *Theory, Culture and Society,* 17.4, 93–117. Accessed 3 March, 2022 at https://www.ios.sinica.edu.tw/people/personal/hlwang/hlwang2000-1.pdf.

Yahoo News, 2 March 2022. "Taiwan President Promises One Month's Salary to Aid Humanitarian Relief Efforts for Ukraine." Located at https://sg.news.yahoo.com/taiwan-president-promises-one-month-121939701.html.

CHAPTER 12

Transnational Conflict, Security, and Militarization

Abstract Conflict, security, and militarization are key aspects of transnational life, reaching beyond traditional conceptions. Anti-Asian and anti-immigrant actions in the United States have illustrated this, and transnational conflict has been common elsewhere in the world (such as in Indonesia). Samuel P. Huntington's *Clash of Civilizations* introduces these ideas. Huntington says that states remain central to human life, but later reverses this. Newcomers may find themselves "groping for groupings," resulting in conflict. Huntington observes a "new era in world politics," but in general sees this in a negative light. People define themselves in terms of their own past and homelands, and do not welcome new peoples. "Cleft countries" of divided peoples are becoming more common. Multiple identities of transnationals may introduce problems as well as benefits. Militarization and transnational conflict may be most common in Africa, but is being seen worldwide, with Taiwan, a militarized country, a prime example. Huntington veers into near-looks at transnational activity as a positive, but falls back on a preferred "Atlanticist" policy of Westernization. We see that transnational affairs are introducing new conceptions and challenges into conflict, security, and military affairs. It is hoped that the transnational community will handle these issues and trials in the best possible ways.

D. Pendery, *Transnational Taiwan*,
https://doi.org/10.1007/978-981-19-4368-3_12

Keywords Conflict · Security and militarization · Cleft countries · Diaspora · Westernization · Civilization · Anti-Asian violence · Africa · Indonesia

The question of security and conflict in terms of transnational life and citizenry must be considered. To be sure such conflicts have arisen many times, and we don't mean only in "traditional" conflicts (that is, wars), but also in localized violence against immigrant groups—we refer specifically to anti-Asian and anti-any immigration reactions of the populace in the United States in recent years—and as well in terms of the conflictive reactions of immigrant populations within their new countries (this may stop short of violence and other such extreme behavior, and simply be sorts of political struggles and rivalries, such as when immigrants demand rights and privileges in newlands). Outbreaks against Chinese immigrants have often been seen in Indonesia (see Amy Chua, *World on Fire*, 2004, for a description of this), and it has been found "that most armed conflicts in Africa have a significant transnational element" (*reliefweb*). I probably don't need to go on, as any number of conflicts, military and local, have taken place in transnational contexts and spheres worldwide for decades and decades.

Other types of this conflict include various foreign and proxy support of conflicts and insurgencies in nations, non-state support of conflict, franchised terrorism, and transnational criminal networks (I will not examine these types of violence and conflict). One observer considers the contrast between "'hard' local territorial [conflict] and… 'soft' transnational extension of ideas," in which we see the key difference we have roughly referred to—actual violence and even bloodshed on the one hand, and the class and competition of ideology and beliefs on the other, and this all can become "incredibly dynamic, adaptable, [and] asymmetric" (*Knowledge Platform*).

Samuel P. Huntington: *E Pluribus Unum*?

At one very high level, I am inclined to view transnational conflict in terms of Samuel P. Huntington's (1927–2008) "Clash of Civilizations" thesis. Now, admittedly, Huntington's theory has come under a great deal of criticism over the years, and it is not taken as seriously now as it was when it caused such a great stir upon publication. I should probably note, outright, that the statist/realist Huntington flatly states in his book, "States are and will remain the dominant entities in world affairs," which seems to remove him from the transnational conversation (34; the word transnational is not even listed in *The Clash of Civilizations* index). "At a basic level," he continues, "the assumptions of the statist paradigm have been true throughout history," and they "thus do not help us to understand how global politics…will differ" from the past into the future (34, slightly reworded).[1] Well clearly, we are looking at a new paradigm as far as transnationalism, and statements like this do not help us much here and now. Nevertheless, we could view all of the migration and immigration we have been considering, from all the different citizens around the world traveling to every other nation, as something of a cultural or "civilizational" consideration (I leave it to the reader to determine how this will impact conflicts in the future, whether seen in Huntington's or another context). To be sure, and as we have considered, the migrants, evacuees, foreigners, and aliens around the world very much bring their home cultures with them when they cross borders, and very much keep their connections to their home countries, no matter how far away they may find themselves. Yes, in newlands the newcomers may find themselves "groping for groupings" (*Clash of Civilizations* 127) but in opposition to Huntington, we for the most part see a positive here.

Huntington calls his thesis a "New Era in World Politics" (19), "an era in which multiple and diverse civilizations will interact, compete, coexist and accommodate each other" (95). Suddenly Huntington is sounding a lot more transnational, and he goes on to make his point clear, and in substantive ways, it sounds very much transnational (Huntington had written about exactly this in his "Transnational Organizations in World Politics," 2011). Huntington states, "People define themselves in terms of ancestry, religion, language, history, values, customs and institutions," which very much sounds like the people we are talking about, although

[1] Huntington later reverses himself, saying states are "suffering losses in sovereignty, functions, and power" (35), that international (transnational?) institutions are now exerting greater power over states, and that we are seeing a "devolution to substate, regional, provincial, and local political entities" (35). States are becoming "increasingly permeable" (35), which seems to hint at a transnational reality.

admittedly this is not Huntington's focus (21).[2] To continue, travelers "identify with cultural groups, tribes, ethnic groups, religious communities, nations, and, at the broadest level, civilizations" (21)—again relevant, though again we differ from what Huntington will find in terms of the meaning of this. In a word, all this complexity, with a reading of these detailed folk features upwards into civilizations, though in some respects opening the door rather widely, does seem to resonate in the terms we have discussed. Huntington observes that "non-Western societies increasingly assert their own cultural values and reject those 'imposed' on them by the West," which has that intolerant touch that Huntington has been criticized for, and although this is a look *within* those societies, their citizenries, and not a look *without* into the transnational world, it nonetheless still has relevance in terms of how those from outside are taking in what they learn and experience in newlands (*Clash of Civilizations* 21–28). And of course, this statement can be seen in light of how travelers retain their original values, carrying them into, reimagining them, and "asserting" them in newlands (and in turn retaining communicative connections to origins), and balancing these opposing and contending views; all said here can be seen simply in terms of political competition and action, such as the abovementioned access to newland rights and privileges. In these respects, Huntington sees how groups from various countries, wherever they might be, "rally to the support of their 'kin countries,'" and, to repeat, we have seen how just this is true among transnationals (28). But all is not well with Huntington. He sees a "challenge" to home cultures coming from "immigrants…who reject assimilation and continue to adhere to and to propagate the values, customs, and cultures of their home societies" (304–305). Well, we have seen how just this is acceptable and true among transnationals, and above Huntington observed how assimilation (actually, "immigration") can result in "a potential source of new vigor and human capital" (304) in newlands. In any case, there has rarely been any notice of transnational peoples refusing to assimilate into new cultures (needless to say, they

[2] Broadly, Huntington refers here to a process of "indigenization" (91–95), whereby many different peoples from around the world are arising, and staking their claims to recognition. With Huntington of course, this is mostly a negative, simply non-Western people taking a stance in opposition to the West. We instead will view such "indigenization" as a process whereby varied peoples do in fact assert their own identities, in normal, generally beneficial ways, in newlands.

normally welcome this). Now all of the above, I should note and most readers are no doubt aware, is taken in a very different direction by Huntington—he later states that "People and countries with different cultures are *coming apart*" (125; italics added), which is now a look *without,* and not *within* interacting peoples in newlands. I will not closely examine Huntington's own theses here, as this is not a critique of Huntington-ism (though it will at times appear to be).

In all we see here, Vaclav Havel has observed that "Cultural conflicts are increasing and are more dangerous today than at any time in history" (*Clash of Civilizations* 28), which perhaps goes a bit far, but can be seen in light of what we are discussing. Huntington himself observes the possibility of conflict in a slightly more transnationalized context when he writes that states "cooperate with and ally themselves with states with similar or common culture and are more often in conflict with countries of different culture" (34). Replace the word "peoples" for "countries" and "states" in this phrase, and the reader can see what I mean. He goes on that conflict can stem from questions of "territory, wealth, and resources, and relative power [and] the ability to impose one's own values, culture, and institution on another group…" (129). These questions could arise and cause conflict among transnational and native peoples in newlands, and we must keep a sharp eye out for this possibility.

In sum, we can see here how transnational peoples in newlands could very well encounter tension, conflict, and reprisals based on their own cultures, which they have taken into new countries (and the reverse, local/native peoples could encounter tension, conflict, and reprisals from transnationals, based on encounters with their own values and cultural principles). People with "shared language, religion, values, institutions and culture" are less likely to be a "threat," Huntington writes (34), which is true enough, but in terms of transnationals, these peoples are in the very process of *engaging with and adopting* the new language, religion, values, institutions, and culture, and thus they are actively avoiding any possibility of threat or conflict. But, needless to say, we cannot avoid exactly what is implied here, as seen in the anti-Asia and anti-other feelings and violence in the United States. A potentially unrecognized problem in all of this, as just noted, is that we may just see the same (in reverse) occurring with transnational peoples, opposing their newland hosts.

Huntington writes how, in some senses, the transnational world might become a "universal civilization" (and recall his "international society"), wherein there may be a "cultural coming together of humanity, and the increasing acceptance of common values, beliefs, orientations, practices, and institutions by peoples throughout the world" (56), which may yield something "better" (the word is mine, not Huntington's). Such a universal acceptance might come about by way of global acceptance of commercial products and consumer goods, the generalized increased interaction of people worldwide, tourism, the universal impact and receipt of certain global media and communications (notably Western), and widespread entertainment sources (again, principally Western). The spread of a "universal language," most likely English (though Chinese is certainly in the running, and it should be noted that in fact the use of English has fallen in recent decades), is not seen as likely (seemingly in opposition to commonly accepted views), and the reappearance of indigenous languages and the global presence of, not least, Chinese, but as well Spanish, French, Arabic, and Russian, indicate something more (and more on such a language with Stephen Toulmin, below). Huntington sees the emergence of such a "civilization" (everything is such with Huntington) as unlikely, and "The evidence simply does not support [such a] liberal, integrationist assumption" (Huntington 67). But this is not to deny that "improvements in transportation and communication technology have...-made it easier and cheaper to move...around the world" [67], and this had led in the transnational direction.

Ultimately, although many a transnational evokes and endorses the idea of a "universal civilization" (the "world citizen" I have referred to), ultimately, "distinctiveness theory holds that people define themselves by what makes them different from others" (*Clash of Civilizations* 67), and it is such "difference," and less any "sameness" that has a larger impact in world affairs. In terms of identity, Huntington aptly puts it that a citizen of Rome may see himself, alternatively, as a "Roman, an Italian, a Catholic, a Christian, a European, a Westerner" (43, and couldn't this be seen as an indicator of a given transnationalism?), and it is these degrees of difference and in a sense, transformation, that influences his decisions about who, what, and where he is (but note that Huntington did not in this quote take it to the universal level, the "world citizen"). Huntington finally says that in fact globalization (he does not mention transnationalism), *exacerbates* (italics Huntington's) feelings of difference across national and civilizational lines, which in turn reduces any feelings of universal humanness (68). We may see here an "us versus them" mentality (very much emphasized by Huntington, and taken in his own direction). In this respect, Huntington, always a bit antagonistic and negative, observes how the us/them, in/out, civilized/barbarian peoples may struggle with feelings of difference (inferiority-superiority), lack of trust, difficulty in communication, and lack of familiarity with newland customs—which are all truths that transnational people handle on a daily basis, and by no means see as insurmountable obstacles! (see 129).[3]

Huntington introduces the idea of "cleft countries" (137; also called "torn countries") wherein conflict among different transnationalities can be severe, and the "fault lines" separating different peoples in newlands can result in "particular problems maintaining [a country's] unity" (137). This in turn gives rise to conflict among groups of differing others. "Deep divisions are...much more likely to emerge within a *cleft country* where large groups belong to different civilizations" (137, italics Huntington's; and we may pause here to reconsider to what extent a given transnational really is a member of this or that "civilization" in Huntington's terms; it seems in some senses that transnational travelers more or less give up just this designation and the nationalistic and jingoistic overtones it carries). Deep divisions may emerge among transnationals and the local populace—suggesting, needless to say, the possibility of conflict and violence—and the two groups may, at worst, take on a view of "We are different people and belong in different places" (*Clash of Civilizations* 138), summed up in the asking of "'Who are we?' 'Where do we belong?' And 'Who is not us?'" (from *Clash of Civilizations* 125). These may become questions of identity in people and nations, which admittedly is a highly important subject (we have mentioned it often), and no doubt does play a strong role in peoples' interactions in Taiwan and worldwide. At a core level, transnational peoples struggle with identity issues as they remake their lives in newlands—often taking on whole new subjectivities/identities (or nationalities) in the process (and we will see this again below, in a conversation with one of my students who has lived in the United States for many years, and in the conclusion to this work). I do not here endorse absolutely the notion that "People define their identity by what they are not" (*Clash of Civilizations* 67), and instead believe that an essentially (though not always) positive process is evoked, in which new sources of identity and community can be enacted, new values and

[3] Note also that Said discusses the "us versus them" mentality, common in imperial culture, saying that such views of identity were "quite settled, clear, unassailably self-evident" (xxv). Such a view of "identity" (quotes Said's) had become the hallmark of both imperialist culture, and the cultures resisting this domination.

morals can be identified with, and new senses of meaning and purpose can be evinced (from *Clash of Civilizations* 97). But again, a struggle remains for transnationals. "In times of rapid social change… [which we may reasonably call the transnational world] established identities dissolve, the self must be redefined, and new identities created" (*Clash of Civilizations* 97, with added text). Nothing wrong with this, simply a truism in the world we are examining.

The question becomes even more complex when we consider *multiple identities,* which perhaps transnational people are most burdened with. "Identification along one dimension may clash with those along a different dimension" writes Huntington (128), and I would not disagree. In these respects, transnational peoples are confronted by a ticklish situation, and various conflicts, internal and external, could arise. In any case, I will not go along with the claim that transnationals (of course the word is not Huntington's) will "distance themselves" (126) from peoples who are different, much less that this is a "zero-sum" choice (130), or that all of these interacting peoples "naturally distrust and see as threats those who are different" (130). Though conflicts among these varying groups, striving for recognition and uniqueness in sometimes amorphous and alienating new social contexts is certainly possible, and often very probable, a more accurate depiction is a view onto how well they normally get along, and how well they solve problems and avoid conflicts, striving toward solidarity, value, morality, social acceptance, common culture, and order (again, not always true, and many times not, with terrible outcomes). These processes of "identity reconstruction," though sometimes painful, usually difficult, prolonged, and interrupted, have proven to be quite "doable" and available to transnational peoples (and by no means "failed" as Huntington writes (*Clash of Civilizations* 139). "Cultural identity" in all of this, is to be sure a "central factor," but not in any way as Huntington posits it (*Clash of Civilizations* 125).

Huntington notes how the United States, possibly more than any other nation, is in danger of such a cleft, forked development, and how minority groups of all sorts (Spanish speakers and Asians, notably, but also blacks and Native Americans, who we don't normally think of as transnational in the respects we have examined [their ancient history aside]), are increasing their populations in the country dramatically. Although there have been signs of conflict between aboriginal Taiwanese and other peoples, for the most part these have not erupted widely, and these people, as noted, generally think of themselves as truly Taiwanese "locals," and thus there is little danger of anything like forked/cleft conflict.

Another important question is militarization of different countries, and how they bring military growth and development into their relations with other states. While statist on the surface, this question can be seen in transnational contexts. Without question, Taiwan is a relatively militarized state in these terms, and engages in various "transnational" relations with other militaries around the world in military matters (just recently, it was announced that Taiwanese non-commissioned officers would be trained in the United States; see "Taiwan to send NCOs to US: source," *Taipei Times*, 15 April 2022). In a word, transnational security challenges in these ways are emerging as critical issues for states worldwide, and perhaps most importantly in the Asia–Pacific region. Varied multifaceted, intersected, and multidimensional threats take place in spheres in which the state is no longer the most important actor in international affairs, which are sometimes called non-international armed conflicts or transnational enemies of a non-state character (Paulus 99). In terms of transnational conflict of the highest order, it has been found that "the traditional dichotomy between international and non-international (internal) armed conflict does not quite match the complexity of modern-day constellations, including, in particular, situations in which non-state groups operate transnationally or across the borders of occupied territories" (Paulus 99). We thus see a new "constellation" of potential transnational conflict, though again much of this might be seen as typical warfare at certain levels, and we must keep in mind the more localized reality of discrimination and violence that takes place against transnational people at homegrown levels (and here again we mention anti-Asian violence seen recently in the United States).

Security issues worldwide "have traditionally been defined in military terms, yet the post-Cold War security landscape contains numerous non-military challenges to security" writes Dupont (no page number). Such non-military considerations have been named by Dupont as overpopulation, deforestation, pollution, global warming, population movements, transnational crime, and new strains of infectious diseases (I will not examine each of these separately here). Dupont argues that such emerging classes of non-military threats are introducing the potential to destabilize societies and polities worldwide, and how such realities are in essence transnational, that is, not solely international. He shows that transnational shifts in military affairs and conflict must be dealt with by governments, nongovernmental organizations, NSAs, and citizenries regionally, and internationally, if conflict is to be circumvented. Collectively, all of this represent a new agenda and poses new challenges for foreign affairs and defense policies in transnational contexts.

In a number of senses, Huntington goes on a negative tear against all the possibilities we have examined, criticizing the very idea of "multiculturalism" being adopted in countries. Readers may debate to what extent transnationalism actually represents "multiculturalism," but it seems to us to be a logical connection, and we might say that the idea is the very essence of transnationalism. Said had himself written of the "new histories" and "new narratives" that comprise multicultural life, and that the "many histories" in the United States are "by no means to be suddenly feared since many of them were always there, and out of them *an* American society and politics...were in fact created" (xxvi, italics in original). Huntington takes no such positive view, and for him, multiculturalists are "very often ethnocentric separatists" who simply reject all that is Western (Arthur Schlesinger Jr. in Huntington 305). In turn, they wish to "divest" home cultures of their very inheritances, and seek "redemptive infusions from non-Western cultures" (305). To this we say, that sounds like an "infusion" that might well bring something great into any new culture. Do not Americans and people in most lands enjoy infusions of other cultures—celebration of Chinese New Year, Cinco de Mayo, Halloween for that matter, foreign cuisines of all kinds, and hey, haven't English speakers been borrowing and using foreign words and phrases for centuries? For Huntington, the idea of multiple cultures sharing experience in newlands is a veritable threat to civilizational existence, "attacking identification," "derailing common culture," and promoting "racial, ethnic, and other subnational...identities and groupings" (from *Clash of Civilizations* 305). Huntington will in large part reverse these views later in the book, though never admitting as much. Any multiculturalism is bound to become "a tangle of squabbling nationalities," bringing nations to "ruin" (as Theodore Roosevelt said, *Clash of Civilizations* 306), and ultimately "promote" diversity rather than unity" (from *Clash of Civilizations* 306). What's wrong with that? we ask (and to be sure nothing like this is taking place in Taiwan). Huntington's focus here is nothing more than an obsessive attachment with "Western culture/civilization" (principally American, that is) and all that is spectacular and awesome about it, "rejecting the siren call of multiculturalism" (307). For Huntington, this idea is an elusive desire to "attach" oneself to a culture that is not actually one's own, which is "precluded" by cultural gaps between any and all cultures. This is to say that transnationalists, who are in the main embracing new cultures, actually "wish to create a country of many civilizations [in other words, not just American]" that will "lack a cultural core" (*Clash of Civilizations* 306). Again, we ask: What's wrong with that, and rather than a set, immovable "core," what is hoped is to create a permeable, flexible, moving, growing, interconnected, communal *new* essence, with multiple nationalities, values, customs, and cultures, all at play. "Are we a Western people or are we something else?" asks Huntington (307), and the question above rests in its stead. I need hardly place Taiwan in the midst of this conflagration, and I am very sure that almost no Taiwanese people, open and open-minded as I have said, would support these views.

Huntington attaches his commentary to a rejection of any idea of "the universality of Western culture" (310; in fact, on objection to the very thing he believes in, though in keeping with his comments about the impossibility of any such culture). That non-Western peoples of any stripe should even think about adopting Western culture is "immoral" (*Clash of Civilizations* 310). I will not pursue this, except to say that if non-Westerners wish to move into such a culture and adopt its values, what's wrong with that? (This same question seems to come up often with Huntington.) And the reverse is true: If Westerners move into non-Western cultures, is that a bad thing? Does anyone think that I, an American in Taiwan, am attempting to "subvert" Taiwanese culture, am "immoral and dangerous" in these respects? (*Clash of Civilizations* 310). In any event, we have already commented extensively on exactly how varied transnational peoples retain links to their home cultures![4] Amidst all this, Huntington announces that "Imperialism is the necessary logical consequence of universalism," which may have been true in ages past, but in any event, has no connection to our idea of transnationalism—which we have never claimed would be "universal" in any case (though ardent

[4] Oddly enough, I have seen that this conception, so important to our overall analysis, is both true and not true in Taiwan. I refer here only to Westerners, who I have noted often seem to maintain connections to their homelands (and indeed many Westerners "parachute" into Taiwan, teach English for a few years, and then disappear back to their native lands). On the other hand, I have observed that many do not maintain very strong connections, and in fact turn against the West and their home countries, a rather misguided and vague attempt to "be Asian" rather than Western, which they reject outright at this point.

transnational proponents would say something like this, and admittedly even my "world citizen" might agree). Ah yes, in the end, we might say, Huntington was right when he said that what nations and peoples and cultures really need to do is "navigate the shallows, endure the miseries, moderate the ventures" of cultural sharing and overlap, which is exactly what transnational peoples do in the world today (*Clash of Civilizations* 311). In the end, Huntington essentially reverses all of this, and though he never speaks of anything exactly like transnationalism, he comes close when he writes that "the world requires acceptance of global multiculturality" [but not multiculturalism?] (318), and of "the attempt to expand the values, institutions, and practices…in common with peoples of [other] civilizations" (320, slightly reworded). Another time Huntington states that "the requisites for cultural coexistence demand a search for what is common to most civilizations" by way of which we "accept diversity, and seek commonalities" (318)—again we see the hint of the transnational in Huntington, which may be unavoidable, and which he even admits is true (again, 318), though not in any positive sense. Finally, at the very end of the book, Huntington goes so far as to say (he in fact "warns"), that the world is entering an "age when different civilizations will have to learn to live side by side in peaceful interchange, learning from each other, studying each other's history and ideals and art and culture, mutually enriching each other's lives" (321).[5] We agree that such a future is on our doorstep in the transnational age in Taiwan, though to be sure Huntington does not go along with any such evaluation. In the final analysis, what he desires is a Western/U.S./European "Atlanticist" policy of cultural coordination, seemingly an embrace of the very civilizational approach he hounds throughout most of the book.

Huntington looks at diasporas, but he does not think much of them. He had earlier in his book noted that "recipient civilizations selectively borrow items from other civilizations, adapt, transform, and assimilate them" (76) into their lives, which sounds like a positive look at "recipient" newlands and those who bring new developments into them. Later though, he notes that "communal conflicts" that "involve groups from different civilizations" have become common around the world (272), and he will link this conflict to diaspora travelers in newlands. Huntington

[5] These words are taken from Lester Pearson (1897–1972), Canadian scholar, statesman, diplomat, and politician, who served as the prime minister of Canada from 1963 to 1968.

finds that these new peoples turn to their "kin countries" for support in conflict, greatly widening the violence and problems (needless to say in opposition to the argument we have presented). He calls these "fault line conflicts" within nations, pitting groups against one another in grinding ways. "In one way or another," he goes on, "diasporas and kin countries have been involved in every fault line war of the 1990s" (273), indicating a reduced view of the value of diasporas (he points out that the Jewish diaspora, as well as the travels of Armenians, Croatians, Chechens, and others have bolstered conflicts). Using electronic communications and other methods, "The commitments of diasporas [to conflict] are reinvigorated and sometimes polarized by constant contact with their former homes; 'former' no longer means what it did" (274, with added text, citing Khaching Tololyan in 1994). Needless to say, this is in opposition to all we have said about just such home contacts, often bolstered by electronic communication. We have noted that conflict is relatively common in transnational contexts, but also that it is generally of a lower level, and of course not often reach levels of warfare. To what extent some of the sources of these larger conflicts are due to transnational diasporas is no doubt debatable, and in any case, at the highest level, with the twentieth-century Asian diasporas to newlands, I am not aware of any such instance (though admittedly there have been some serious conflicts, such as that pitting Chinese immigrants and Indonesians).

I have gone farther afield in this analysis based on Samuel P. Huntington. Readers who are familiar with Taiwan life and culture can take this analysis into their scope, and understand how it would all transpire in Taiwan, and what ramifications these ideas and issues would have here. From my own perspective, very much a transnational in Taiwan, I have not often seen conflict among Taiwanese people and other transnationals, though there have been questions, as noted above. There has been talk of "egregious injustices" faced by migrants in Taiwan, and a U.S. State Department report stated that "migrant workers in Taiwan are generally exploited…and commonly subjected to poor [and harsh] working conditions" (*Taipei Times*, unsigned editorial). I refer here principally to overseas workers who have relocated to Taiwan, mostly from other SE Asian nations, which we have looked at above. As for the rest of "us" (I should perhaps say "them"), the other foreigners in Taiwan (many from Western countries), I am sure that not a single one would complain about the treatment he or she has received, and the general welcoming quality of life in Taiwan.

In conclusion, "Cultural commonalities and differences shape the interests, antagonisms, and associations" of all peoples, which can be seen as more than relevant in what we are observing (*Clash of Civilizations* 29; note that Huntington referred to "states" here, not "peoples" as I have written, state-centered realist as he is). "The local conflicts most likely to escalate into broader wars are those between groups and states from different civilizations" (29), which is partially (but not entirely) state-centric, but is again relevant as far as the cultural groupings and associations we are examining, meaning, again, that conflict is very possible in transnational contexts (though as noted rarely if ever erupting into anything like wars; of course, Huntington and this writer are simply observing these realities from different perspectives).

We see in the above that transnational affairs are introducing new conceptions and challenges into the control and administration of conflict, security, and developments in military affairs. Taiwan, as a firmly militarized society with a large transnational population and not a few connections to other nation's militaries, has much at stake here. It shall be hoped that the transnational community will handle these issues and trials in the best possible ways, and continually reduce the threats and difficulties in newlands around the world.

References

Dupont, Alan, 2001. *East Asia Imperilled: Transnational Challenges to Security*. Cambridge UP. Located at https://books.google.com.tw/books. The entire Internet address is not included here and this book can be found at books.google.com.

Huntington, Samuel P., 1996. *The Clash of Civilizations and the Remaking of World Order*. Simon and Schuster.

Knowledge Platform Security & Rule of Law, 2017. "Understanding Types of Transnational Conflict for Coherent Policy." Located at https://www.kpsrl.org/blog/understanding-types-of-transnational-conflict-for-coherent-policy.

Paulus, Andreas, Mindia Vashakmadze, 2009. "Asymmetrical War and the Notion of Armed Conflict—A Tentative Conceptualization." *International Review of the Red Cross*, 91.873, March 2009. Located at https://www.corteidh.or.cr/tablas/R23029.pdf.

reliefweb, 2019. "Transnational Conflict in Africa (10 October 2019)." Located at https://reliefweb.int/report/world/transnational-conflict-africa-10-october-2019.

Said, Edward W., 1993–1994. *Culture and Imperialism*. Vintage Books.

Taipei Times, Staff Writer, 15 April 2022. "Taiwan to Send NCOs to US: Source." Located at https://www.taipeitimes.com/News/taiwan/archives/2022/04/15/2003776646.

Taipei Times, Unsigned Editorial, 26 March, 2022. "Taiwan Should Lead on Migrant Rights." Located at https://taipeitimes.com/News/editorials/archives/2022/03/26/2003775463.

CHAPTER 13

Stephen Toulmin's View on Transnationalism

Abstract Stephen Toulmin has a positive view of transnationalism, in contrast to Samuel P. Huntington. He examines Cartesian philosophy and its wide impact globally, and sees that it is a negative, certainty-based, ultra-rationalist view that limits a wider view onto humanity, taking in the ambiguity and uncertainty normal in human life and interaction. Transnational institutions and individuals are very much in contrast to this. Descartes and his followers dominated philosophy until the twentieth century, even up to the twenty-first century, but new understanding of the ambiguity of life and a "skeptical tolerance" have gradually become more acceptable, leading to the onset of transnational ideas and peoples. A look back to the "Renaissance humanists" of the seventeenth century is necessary, and an embrace of their more forgiving and accepting worldviews.

Keywords Cartesian philosophy · Transnationalism · Kaleidoscopic diversity · Renaissance humanists · Skeptical tolerance · Diversity · Colonialism · Imperialism · Michel de Montaigne · Gottfried Wilhelm Leibniz · Global language · European Union · India · Sovereign nation · Loyalty · Ambiguity · Horizon of expectation

D. Pendery, *Transnational Taiwan*,
https://doi.org/10.1007/978-981-19-4368-3_13

Stephen Toulmin (1922–2009) has considered all of these issues, much more, and transnationality particularly, in his *Cosmopolis: The Hidden Agenda of Modernity*. His analysis takes us up a few steps, into a more ethereal view of the importance of these ideas, but is very valuable. Toulmin's book is, at the highest level, a sustained attack on Cartesian philosophy, with its focus on a given "certainty" in life and letters. This inevitable certitude can enter into all views of the world and its peoples, their ideas and conceptions. It is a theorized view onto life, timeless, universal, ultra-rational/positivist, which seeks to remove any doubts, ambiguities, tolerance, true skepticism, and falls short of the "kaleidoscopic diversity" of existence (Toulmin 26), as well as any contextual understanding of problems and vagaries in life. Before Descartes, the "Renaissance humanists" ruled the day, and they took a more open-minded look at life, allowing for just these qualities in their worldviews, a "skeptical tolerance" (Toulmin 25) that "[r]eflect[ed] on the detailed nature and circumstances of concrete human actions" (Toulmin 27), with an eye toward "the significance of local diversity, the relevance of particularity, and the rhetorical power of oral reasoning" (Toulmin 34). Associated with the Cartesian rationalism in philosophy and letters, was a similar view of the nation-state—that is, sovereign, rational, self-sustaining political units, independent of any true contextual relations, seen in the theory of John Locke and his followers, which "devalued practice and insisted…on the needs to find foundations for knowledge that were clear, distinct and certain" (Toulmin 70). Perhaps needless to say, even in that day, there was recognition of the (ambiguous) transnational, though this might have principally been understood in terms of arbitrary colonialism and imperious imperialism, and the travels from homelands into newlands that such activities manifested. Such Cartesian *theoretical* conceptions became the order of the day for centuries after, drifting away from the skeptical, pragmatic, "honest examination of experience" (Toulmin 70), and into a *universal philosophy* and *theoretical* conception of human affairs that ignored the key practical-minded points (Toulmin 34). Something new is to be sure now required, Toulmin tells us, a retreat from stark rationalism/positivism, and "[t]he times that we live in demand institutions of new and more functional kinds: institutions that overlap national boundaries and serve *trans*national social and economic needs" (Toulmin 7, italics in original). A new Michel de Montaigne-esque (not Cartesian) "skepticism" is needed, which asks the right questions and seeks the contextual answers needed in the twenty-first century (we often think of Descartes as essentially "skeptical," but as noted what is meant here is the skepticism of a Montaigne, whereby a given "horizon of expectations," and a "practical modesty" and "intellectual freedom" are explored for actual—not necessarily "certain"—meaning [Toulmin 42]). Descartes desired to "start from scratch," and eliminate the "modest skepticism of the humanists" (Toulmin 81), into a position of "systematic doubt" that was "universal" and "timeless" (Toulmin 82–83). At the highest level, these views embraced knowledge and understanding in strictly written (as opposed to oral) terms; moved from "the particular to the universal"; from the "local to the general"; and from the "timely to the timeless" (Toulmin *passim*). This all dehumanized intellectual pursuits and qualities in fundamental ways. A move to the transnational, as we will see below, may be just the answer that is needed to back away from this lack of true human comprehension.

We might note here that a follower of Descartes, the German Gottfried Wilhelm Leibniz, though just as ensconced in the ultra-rational worldview, also saw the possibility of a *characteristica universalis*, that is, a "universal/global" language that would "serve wonderfully in communication among various peoples" (Leibniz in Toulmin 100). This sounds like a good idea (similar in some respects to Huntington's thinking), and could very possibly be a sort of evocation of transnationalism, connecting people of different societies, languages, and worldviews. We have, of course, considered just this in the above text, and to be sure the idea of a "world language" has been a hot topic for quite some time now. Leibniz's proposition was never to be, and no such universal language has ever been created, or linked people across all borders in the ways he envisioned. Leibniz always saw his play as a Cartesian entry into the ultra-rational, though perhaps it could have had wider significance, and is something we are still considering today. English is probably the closest we have come to any such global language to date, and to be sure English has linked many different people around the world (though, again, Chinese is not far behind). There is however a given negative to the spread of English, as it was often used in very discriminatory and domineering ways in the eras of colonialism and imperialism. How any such language could or would be used in the future transnational world is still something of an open question.

In some senses, the European Union (EU) might be seen as one of the premier functioning, modern transnational entities. It can be said that the EU's political, social, and economic institutions and policies transcend nation-states, proper, and have higher aims of cooperation and human development. To be sure, it is a largely cooperative amalgamation, "a distinct creature of transnational law" (Fichera 1103), which has in essence brought together the "united states of Europe"—we might note that the EU has 23 official languages. Toulmin observes that the states of the EU have proven "unexpectedly adaptable" to challenge and change, and in the main "institutional structures are less fixed" (206), which has turned a group of once-suspicious neighbors into "a political unit with the power to command common loyalties" (206). The EU, Toulmin writes, may be in a position to "disperse authority and adapt it more discerningly and precisely," in order to meet "the needs of local areas and communities" and perform "wider transnational functions" (206). There are more than a dozen transnational cooperation areas across the EU, with these projects developing and implementing plans addressing education and research, environment and climate change, water resources, digital connectivity, sustainable transport; regional development, labor markets, cultural heritage, tourism development, and governance. This might all be viewed as one essence of transnational governance among groups of emigres and immigrants, travelers and new-arrivals, from and in different nations. Above this, the need for the participation of non-national, subnational, transnational, international, and multinational organizations will be necessary—which might stray a bit from that which is transnational, proper, but is in keeping with all that we have examined (from Toulmin 207). Toulmin goes on to look at India, which has created less a unified "nation" than a "confederation of nations that gain more than they lose [by] staying in the union" (207). We can see such "gains" being taken in my transnational peoples, existing as nations within nations worldwide today. India has become a "sprawling, heterogeneous commonwealth" (207), which we might well say of any other transnationalized nation worldwide. The EU and India may look very different on the outside, but in fact they both take essentially transnational approaches to the governance of their citizens, whichever nations they may be from.

In what might be seen in a similar light, former Taiwan vice president Annette Lu (呂秀蓮) recently proposed a model of "cross-strait integration" to bring China and Taiwan closer together, calling the idea an EU-style bloc that could reduce tension and bring the two sides of the Taiwan Strait closer together. Lu's idea appears in some respects "transnational," and is a step away from "unification" of Taiwan and China (which would lead to only one nation remaining), although Lu's idea might be seen broadly in terms of my *UM* noted above (or simply an EU, as she says), it is in fact probably largely state-centered, simply China and Taiwan attempting to *be* China and Taiwan, once again in keeping with the usual ideas in Taiwan. Critics called the idea "far out" and "out of date," they in the main reflecting statist and largely anti-China positions, in keeping with what is common in Taiwan politics. It's been said already: As transnational as Taiwan is and can be, the nation often falls back on statist sovereignty and autonomy as its focus (from Pan).

To return to our focus, we are, as often noted, of late seeing an essential delegitimization of the sovereign "nation," and an opening into trans-, dia-, and interconnected human life and society. Of course, to say again, in some senses this is not quite true—the sovereign nation does appear to be continuing in the twenty-first century, and we have seen countless examples of just such entities, on the one hand, very much taking part in transnational activity, but on the other, causing nothing but trouble in the world, engaging in ultra-nationalist, authoritarian, jingoistic, and despotic/fascistic behavior. On a more positive note, "The question [is] no longer whether…the whole world [will] create transnational institutions at all: the only practical questions [are] how soon those institutions [will] be set up, what forms they [will] take, and which functions they [will] take over from the omnipresent sovereign nation-state" (Toulmin 160). Toulmin is speaking our language, and we must, in a word, unlearn our dependence on nation-states (and for that matter any other politically defined territory) as monolithic, autonomous entities with ultimate control over any and all citizens and/or visitors within their borders, and seek a more limited model, a move into "subnational, transnational, [non-national], [international], [post-national], or multinational institutions and procedures" (Toulmin 193, with added text). We may find that such entities and institutions will yield a new brand of common loyalty to the powers that be, and more importantly, to the peoples that comprise these domains. "[W]e need to disperse authority and adapt it more discerningly and precisely…[to] the needs of local areas and communities…to wider transnational formations," yielding "transnational networks monitoring national governments" (Toulmin 206). These units of governance, institutions, and new legalities will "restrain the ambitions or curb the actions of…self-willed sovereign nations"—and oh how that could yield a better, more cooperative, more harmonious world—while "restoring humanity to its proper place" with "a renewed toleration of diversity, ambiguity and uncertainty" (Toulmin 152–153).

Professor Sanjoy Bannerjee, cited above, views how Taiwan fits into a transnational context within the Bay Area in California, where "Toulmin's notion of cosmopolitan states [has seen] a nascent flourishing." He notes that "Taiwan…can carry Toulmin's banner. It can lead toward a more cosmopolitan global governance by carving out a place for itself."

Toulmin has given us a vision of something better, the elements of which we can already see emerging all around the "globalized" world. Yes, in this world we will face much "uncertainty and ambiguity," but it is just such qualities of the human race that we would expect, qualities both concrete and complex which we, in the main, welcome (Toulmin 175). A new "horizon of expectation" (Toulmin uses the phrase often)[1] presents us with new possibilities, and as Toulmin would hope, very ***human, contextual, essentially skeptical, modest, local, particular*** possibilities, an embrace of pluralism in the next age of modernity. We must move away from "***foundationalism***—i.e., the search for a permanent and unique set of authoritative principles for human knowledge" (much less human polity), toward a transnational moment of "intellectual honesty, uncertainty, and toleration" (Toulmin 174, italics in original), all within a transnational world of "interdependency, cultural diversity and historical change" (Toulmin 184). We look forward to just this in our new connected world.

References

Bannerjee, Sanjoy, Professor, San Francisco State University, personal communication with author.

Fichera, Massimo, Oreste Pollicino, 2019. "The Dialectics Between Constitutional Identity and Common Constitutional Traditions: Which Language for Cooperative Constitutionalism in Europe?", *German Law Journal,*

[1] "The strength of well-formed 'horizons of expectations'" writes Toulmin, "is not that they generate accurate forecasts to serve as a theoretical basis for the practical politics of the future." Instead, they "foresee…the limits within which available human futures lie." These are futures we can "actively create," all of which sounds like what transnational peoples themselves foresee and aim for (2).

Cambridge UP, pp. 1097–1118. Located at https://www.cambridge.org/core/services/aop-cambridge-core/content/view/E8D1FE181EB6A389ED739155A8F3BB80/S2071832219000828a.pdf/the-dialectics-between-constitutional-identity-and-common-constitutional-traditions-which-language-for-cooperative-constitutionalism-in-europe.pdf.

Pan, Jason, 2022. "Former VP Lu suggests Taiwan-China federation," *Taipei Times,* 8 May 2022.

Toulmin, Stephen, 1992. *Cosmopolis: The Hidden Agenda of Modernity*, U of Chicago P.

CHAPTER 14

Transnational Education

Abstract Following is a look at the many students traveling to newlands for training. I will focus on Taiwanese students studying abroad. Looks at educational collaboration at international levels will be taken, as well as the emergence of cooperative educational provision through varied education institutions, and the development of borderless education. Consideration in Taiwan of a "brain-drain," and a "net gain" in terms of expertise acquired through international education will be examined. Analysis of Taiwanese students as key to the Taiwan diaspora. Consideration of distance education in terms of main subjects. Taiwan's education system has been internationalizing and improving dramatically, with schools and hubs opened and recognized worldwide.

Keywords Transnational education · Taiwanese students · Overseas students · Social impact

Transnational education and mobility among students and academics may be a given, considering how many students are traveling to newlands for training.[1] In 2019, there were over six million international students, up

[1] Adachi, from above, notes that "numerous Kubo young people have gone abroad to Japan and the United States for higher study or internships" (65).

D. Pendery, *Transnational Taiwan*,
https://doi.org/10.1007/978-981-19-4368-3_14

from two million in 2000 (from Wikipedia, "International Student"). Above we noted the number of Taiwanese students studying abroad. The concept is collecting and facilitating a huge new group of students who are absorbing and disseminating knowledge beyond the geographical boundaries of their homelands. It is all leading to the development of new pedagogies, instruction, and information and communication networks, providing opportunities and possibilities for:

- Educational collaboration and cooperation at international levels
- The emergence of cooperative educational provision through higher and lower education institutions
- The development of borderless education.

As noted, Taiwan is very much a part of these exciting new educational developments. Taiwan has seen a great deal of its overseas-trained students actually return to the nation, the reverse of a "brain-drain," and instead a "net gain" in terms of expertise (notably in science and technology). In a word, the return of many skilled students and emigrants has significantly boosted the country's development. Students who have sought education and employment abroad, in many ways the core of the Taiwan twentieth-century diaspora, have created an interface with the global economy, while enhancing Taiwan's manufacturing base and industries, and this has been promoted by Taiwanese educational policy. The contribution of this internationally acquired knowledge base—"through both the physical return of migrants and their participation from overseas—has been promoted by the government itself through policies centered on the Taiwanese diaspora" (O'Neil, no page number). O'Neil also notes how these policies "focused on providing strong universal basic education and vocational programs as demanded by the domestic labor market" (O'Neil). Migration itself "can provide a 'brain reserve,'" and Taiwanese students living overseas "provided advice from afar and returned to meet...-growing demand" in technological industries (O'Neil). Such industries are, needless to say, a very strong area in Taiwan.

With its support of the educational diaspora, Taiwan benefited from its own emigrants, many of them students studying abroad, and in turn often encouraged their return to Taiwan. Taiwanese emigrants (some having returned, some remaining overseas) have new knowledge, skills, and a greater international understanding and language skills, creating a beneficial circle system, as we have described it.

To return, transnational education can include courses of study or educational services (including those stemming from distance education, though transnational education goes much further than just this) in which the learners and teachers are located in countries different from those in which the awarding institution is based. What is found are educational experiences in which learners in one nation work with educational providers in different countries, creating an elastic, upward looking, and quite transnational learning environment. This is related to the general idea of internationalization in higher education, mobility of academics and students, and institutions operating in independent ways across borders of national authority. At present, transnational education is principally being conveyed by developed and technologically advanced countries that have better learning resources and capacity to accept students from all over the world. Transnational education is expanding globally, not least because of the rise of distance education in the COVID age. Such an educational methodology can embrace and train students internationally, and new information and communication technologies are facilitating the advance and promotion of students in a global educational environment. There must be a concentrated effort to ensure outstanding values and worldwide acceptance and adoption of new standards and high quality in transnational education in the future (from Hussain).

Taiwan to be sure can meet these requirements and expectations, and the country's educational system has been internationalizing and improving dramatically in recent decades. As recently as March 2022, Taiwan had launched 45 Taiwan Centers for Mandarin Learning in the United States and Europe, a true transnational linguistic step. The Ministry of Education (MOE) has launched its Higher Education SPROUT Project (Sustained Progress and Rise of Universities in Taiwan), which aims to enhance the quality of universities, encourage multi-faceted development, enable universities to achieve international competitiveness, and construct leading research centers. The MOE has also sought to recruit renowned professors, scholars, and researchers from overseas, attain membership in international organizations, exchange faculty, student and researchers with international universities, and organize symposiums, forums, fairs and conferences worldwide. Since 2001, Taiwan has signed bilateral education agreements with 15 countries, five in Asia. The country has sought to create an East Asian higher education hub in Taiwan, promote talent circulation in response to regional education needs, develop world-class universities (many Taiwan universities have climbed higher and higher on international scales), enable new scholarship programs for local and foreign students, and expand the recruitment of international students—all of which of course we have seen is true in Taiwan (from Taiwan Ministry of Education, and Lin).

The introduction of a 12-year children's educational system, while not transnational, was an important step. I have examined Taiwanese students studying abroad above (as a reminder, in academic year 2019/20, approximately 71,488 students from Taiwan studied in different countries around the world [*Statista*]), and just as important are the new foreign students who are arriving in Taiwan in force. Up to 10% of all students in Taiwan (over 100,000) are now from other countries. I myself have experienced just this, with many of my students at National Taiwan University of Science and Technology (NTUST) of Indonesian, Vietnamese and Chinese origin. My students will have much more to say in "My Taiwanese Students speak" below.

In a word, Taiwan is no doubt inter/transnationalizing its own educational methodologies and systems dramatically, and the travels of Taiwanese students to foreign educational institutions, and the arrival of foreign students in Taiwan is a grand move into a new educational transnationalism. Such interaction is truly a wonderful thing in Taiwan.

References

Adachi, Nobuko, guest editor, 2010. *East Asian Transnational Migrants and Culture in a Global World. Encounters*, fall 2010.

Lin, Arianna Fang-Yu, 2020. "Internationalization initiatives of Taiwan's higher education: a stepping stone to regional talent circulation or reproduction of unbalanced mobility scheme?" *Initiatives of Taiwan's Higher Education*, 69. Located at https://www.emerald.com/insight/content/doi/10.1108/HEED-06-2020-0017/full/pdf.

Ministry of Education, Taiwan, "Higher Education SPROUT Project." Located at https://sprout.moe.edu.tw/SproutWeb/Home/Index/en.

O'Neil, Kevin, 2003. "Brain Drain and Gain: The Case of Taiwan," Migration Policy Institute. Accessed 2 March 2022 at https://www.migrationpolicy.org/article/brain-drain-and-gain-case-taiwan.

Statista. "Number of students from Taiwan studying abroad in academic year 2019/20, by major destination countries." Located at https://www.statista.com/statistics/1092368/taiwan-students-studying-abroad-by-destination-country/.

Wikipedia. "International Student." Located at https://en.wikipedia.org/wiki/International_student.

CHAPTER 15

My Taiwanese Students Speak

Abstract Included are discussions with a number of Taiwanese students, including one who has been educated, lived, and worked in the United States for many years. This student provides insight into transnational experience. Other works were written by current Taiwanese students, commenting on the meaning and importance of transnationalism in life.

Keywords Taiwanese students · Transnationalism · United States · Taiwan

Cerbrina Chou was a student I had in the English department at Shih Hsin University some 20 years ago. She launched a true transnational existence, moving to and obtaining her master's degree in the United States, and then taking a job as a teacher at Chemeketa Community College in Salem, Oregon. She has primarily lived in the United States since her early 20s, now half her life (she lived in Taiwan for a time during the pandemic). She says she has seen "different world views" during her transnational life.

Chou tells me "I always felt that I can fit in easily. It is so diverse here in America and the country is built upon immigrants." She notes, however, that "It takes a lot of time to understand a country and the US is *huge*."

D. Pendery, *Transnational Taiwan*,
https://doi.org/10.1007/978-981-19-4368-3_15

She observed that when she lived in California, there were many Asians nearby, and she could commonly speak Mandarin. In other parts of the country, however, there were fewer Asians, and having to speak English could be a challenge. "I did feel that my English was not good enough compared to colleagues," she says, "so I was fairly quiet in meetings." She adds, "I know the struggle of being an immigrant here. The US is so big and divided."

Chou in some ways feels divided herself. She still speaks Chinese to friends and family, "I'm not that American" she says, but as well, after 20 years overseas, "I can't say I'm foreign anymore." At a yet higher level, she says that "I go back and forth. I struggle in terms of the political ideology of being Chinese or [being] Taiwanese." This separated, in some sense alienated conception is something that many Taiwanese have struggled with.[1] Leo Lin, my student at NTUST, voiced a similar thought, saying "China's political and military oppression of Taiwan causes a lack of national recognition deep in my mind."

Chou tells me that when she taught intercultural communication in Chemeketa, she often shared Taiwanese culture with her students. She has since become a U.S. citizen, the ultimate transnational step. "Essentially, I feel like no country has the best system and no culture is the best," she says. "All I can take from living in both countries is I take advantage of living in each place and try not to complain so much about the flaws of each place."

Ian Shih, a 2022 student in a writing class at National Taipei University of Business (NTUB), told me that in terms of the transnational,

[1] And I truly mean "struggle," not least politically in terms of the two major parties (the Kuomintang and the Democratic Progressive Party), whose politicians are, or are viewed as, "pro-China," "pro-unification," and the like (the KMT), or generally "pro-Taiwan" and "pro-independence" (the DPP). As well, a fair number of now-older Taiwanese, sometimes disparagingly called the wàishěngrén (外省人) or "mainlanders," actually came from China, after the conclusion of the Chinese Civil War in 1949. And of course, a majority of Taiwan's current population does have linkages, ancestry and family in China. According to estimates, "over 95% of Taiwan's population of 23.4 million consists of Han Chinese" (from Wikipedia, "Taiwanese people"). No doubt it's true that waves of immigration have long come from China into Taiwan. This indicates the strong connection between the two countries, whatever differences and conflicts there may be. As well, in this respect, the common Mandarin language links the two sides very closely. Ultimately, many Taiwanese, as we see with my students, wrestle with these realities, while they are also drawn to Taiwanese identity, proper, and in turn the idea of Taiwanese independence from China, at all costs.

"the first word that comes to my mind is international," perhaps stating a truism. In this trans-/inter-world, "communicating with foreigners is utterly important." Ian told me of a South African classmate he had in college, and "by using English to communicate with her, we could understand the cultural differences between Taiwan and South Africa and my horizons were broadened." Thus, though not an overseas traveler, Ian had a true transnational experience, himself speaking with another transnational subject. Other students also told me of this South African, and how the necessity to use English with her had opened them to new transnational experience.

Jessica Huang, a student in the same class, observed that she has communicated with exchange students at NTUB, and "I think they are brave and they need to adapt to a new environment and solve problems by themselves." Transnational people, whether Taiwanese or visiting foreigners, "broaden [their] horizons [and] connect with the world," she added. Transnational peoples "need to force [themselves] to be more outgoing, so [they] won't feel isolated and lonely. Since you are alone in a foreign country, you have to adapt to local lifestyles." But ideally, "you can share your culture with others," and "living in a foreign country, one learns to be independent, and to compromise and adapt to changes during the journey." Huang has identified several key aspects and challenges of the transnational life here.

To wrap up the views of my students in the same class at NTUB, I liked Vivian Xu's take on transnationalism's links and how people are "turning over a new leaf," she seeing that: "When people involve in the concept of transnationalism, they also stimulate the working in globalization. For example, emigrants emigrate from their home country to the host country to open a restaurant with the specialties of the home country, and in this way, people in the host country have the opportunities to taste and understand the other countries' characteristics without really going abroad. It's a win-win situation not only for the immigrants or emigrants to broaden their horizons but also for the different countries to absorb the advantages or skills from other countries and maintain a peaceful relationship." Leo Lin, my student at NTUST, simply noted that the experience of the many migrants, travelers, refugees, etc., can be summed up in a Chinese saying that reads, "the moon looks fuller overseas" (外國的月亮比較圓, wàiguó de yuèliàng bǐjiào yuán) indicating how we all must take a second look during our travels and migrations, to sense and determine just what is best and most authentic.

To sum up, I turn to a longer reflection, written by William Chen, also my student at NTUST. Chen reflects thoughtfully on the advantages and disadvantages of all we have examined, and concludes with an obliging consideration on the world at large, and how we are all taken in to these ideas of excursion, place, comity, and identity.

> On July 20th, 1969, when Neil Armstrong set foot on the moon, the world cheered. "We did it!"—not "America did it," but, "We did it." This was a moment that the world shared, and proof that when humans come together as a species, great accomplishments can be achieved. Virtually no country in the world is truly self-sufficient, and the many problems of the world are not solvable by any one nation. Transnationalism is not just some new concept, it is the way of the future.
>
> We have been taught the concept of a "Global Village" since elementary school, and I think transnationalism has many similarities with this. In the age of the Internet, it's easy to the point of being unavoidable to interact with people halfway across the globe. Despite some obvious flaws, like the spreading of misinformation, having the ability to connect with anyone anywhere is certainly a good thing. Taiwan, however lovely, is undeniably small. To build a life of our own, most of us have to look beyond our borders, to be a part of some larger chain. From seeking opportunities through international work in the world, to buying groceries around the corner, our daily lives are filled with elements from all over the world.

Very much thanks to these students, who have made such a valuable contribution to this work by way of writings and interviews I conducted with them.

Reference

Wikipedia. "Taiwanese People." Located at https://en.wikipedia.org/wiki/Taiwanese_people.

CHAPTER 16

Conclusion

Abstract Here is a final overview and discussion of my own transnational experience and life in Taiwan, including having a daughter here. Final look at poetry by Taiwanese Fang Tzu Chang. Look at teaching as providing transnational experience in terms of language and student behavior. Final look at Norwegian monk Hugo of St. Vincent, and Said's final evaluation of transnational activity. Final consideration by Pendery of transnational life, looking at work of John Winthrop.

Keywords Transnational life in Taiwan · Fang Tzu Chang · John Winthrop · Hugo of St. Vincent

How much we have seen in this analysis! And what exciting possibilities this introduces into life in Taiwan, and globally. A new transnational world, a world of cooperative, interactive, trans-social possibilities seems not only within reach, but to be taking place at this moment, and introducing new worldviews into our comprehension. I need not here repeat all the details of this reality, which we have examined in this work. Instead, I will reflect on my own transnational experience living in Taiwan and see if it perhaps sheds a bit of light into what are perhaps some dim corners. I function as a "transnational" in Taiwan by being a foreigner (we the wàiguó rén, 外國人, as we are called), an expatriate who interacts with

D. Pendery, *Transnational Taiwan*,
https://doi.org/10.1007/978-981-19-4368-3_16

the local people all the time—mostly in English. Yes, I have to admit that I have not fully mastered Chinese, and that is a step back from true transnational experience and proficiency. Taiwanese people reciprocate my own transnational feelings, however, in that almost all can speak English (for better or worse). To top all of this off, I have a bilingual five-year-old daughter at home, with both Taiwanese and U.S. citizenship—how transnational is that!?!

I was thumbing through *somewhere we belong* by Taiwanese poet Fang Tzu Chang and came across a piece that caught my attention, seeming to evince a transnational feeling. Fang herself is perhaps not a transnational poet, per se, her work tends more toward the introspective. She does, however, express some mobile ideas in her work—"I know you have been here" (13), "Who would mind the mud on the shoe toes?" (27), "Who doesn't want to take off?" (29), "Uprooted / Trampled / Yet persisting in growing deep into the earth— / Extending our vessels of roots" (42), "As wide as the Pacific / The road to Language / Lies in every sound of prayers" (91), "As a stone paved in the homeland / Just step on me" (50).

This work was translated by my friend, Charles Chen. Chen himself is not fully transnational, he has never lived overseas, but he has traveled often. More to the point, his passion for English letters and literature, and his experience translating works from Chinese to English, brings a transnational vibe into his life, crossing cultures, and languages.

This piece, "Sound of Water," by Fang, gives rise to feelings of struggle, "flowing far and nigh," transgressions, moving "back and forth," and finally, "migration."

> Let you stir waves, in which I flow far and nigh—
> I raise my hands, shouting for help, while getting closer.
> Perhaps you want me to drift,
> Perhaps you want me to struggle.
> So hard and very hard,
> I swim back into your eyes—
> Swim back…swim back…
> Back and forth—
> In migration. (137)

Teaching in an English program at NTUB creates a transnational "vibe," an empathy, a concord, a bit of passion that extends outward into all the people I meet, in that the study of foreign language is a "reach across borders" at all times (and we saw this in the student comments above. My study of Chinese (I keep trying) takes me much deeper into this "trans-" worldview. Simply the fact that I traveled half way around the world and relocated here—the alien, the expatriate, the foreigner—has thrust me into a specific transnational border crossing. And here the "ex-" of one nominal conception (expatriate), and the "trans-" of another (transnational), have similar connotations in this expansive and expanding worldview. My identity, my now "being Taiwanese" (and believe me reader, you don't know the whole of this reality), has altered my prior national conscience and consciousness, and introduced me into this new, transnational world, overflowing with new languages, experiences, connections, contacts, acquaintances, associates, networks, systems, arteries, circuitries, complexities…all at a booming, burgeoning, breakneck pace…all in a newfound checkerboard, fabric, compass, arena…of life, growth, heart and soul…. It all offers this and so much more!

I am drawn to the words of Hugo of St. Vincent, the twelfth-century Norwegian monk:

> It is therefore, a source of great virtue for the practiced mind to learn, bit by bit, first to change about in visible and transitory things, so that afterwards it may be able to leave them behind altogether. The person who finds his homeland sweet is a tender beginner; he to whom every soil is as his native one is already strong; but he is perfect to whom the entire world is as a foreign place. The tender soul has fixed his love on one spot in the world; the strong person has extended his love to all places; the perfect man has extinguished his. (in Said 335)

Said goes on that "No one today is purely *one* thing. Labels like Indian, or woman, or Muslim, or American are not more than starting-points, which if followed into actual experience for only a moment are quickly left behind…just as human beings make their own history, they also make their cultures and ethnic identities. No one can deny the persisting continuities of long traditions, sustained habitations, national languages, and cultural geographies, but there seems no reason except fear and prejudice to keep insisting on their separation and distinctiveness, as if that was all human life was about… It is more rewarding – and more difficult – to think concretely and sympathetically, contrapuntally, about others than only about 'us'" (336, italics in original).

Said adds (these words are actually found at the start of his work), that as we enter the twenty-first century, "there has been a gathering awareness nearly everywhere of the lines *between* cultures, the divisions and differences that not only allow us to discriminate one culture from another, but also enable us to see the extent to which cultures are humanly made structures of both authority and participation, benevolent in what they include, incorporate, and validate, less benevolent in what they exclude and demote." Such "hybrid historical and cultural experiences are...[f]ar from being unitary or monolithic or autonomous things, [and they] actually assume more 'foreign' elements, alterities, differences than they consciously exclude. Who...can confidently separate out [given national/transnational entities and configurations] from present actualities, and who...can draw a clear circle around [these same national/transnational entities and configurations]?" (Said 15, reworded; italics in original).

In my own view, expressed in "Taiwan a 'city on a hill' for Asia," in the *Taipei Times* (2 April 2019), I wrote that "every man might have need of others, and from hence they might be all knit more nearly together" (by John Winthrop, "A Model of Christian Charity," 1630), an indication of all the connectivity I have examined. Taiwan, in a word, has exhibited just such binding and attachment to peoples and countries all over the world, and to repeat, this transnational foreigner in Taiwan has seen and experienced this. I hope that I will continue to meet and interact with any number of others who hopefully, proudly, expectantly, apprehensively, and always enthusiastically find ourselves in this new transnational space of existence. Thank you.

References

Fang Tzu Chang, 2018. *somewhere we belong*. Translated by Charles Chen. Show Art Publishing.

Pendery, David, 2019 "Taiwan a 'city on a hill' for Asia," *Taipei Times*, 2 April, 2019.

Said, Edward W., 1993–1994. *Culture and Imperialism.* Vintage Books.

Sources Cited

Academy for Cultural Diplomacy. "Chinese Diaspora Across the World: A General Overview." Accessed 21 February 2022 at https://www.culturaldiplomacy.org/academy/index.php?chinese-diaspora#:~:text=Chinese%20migrants%20amount%20to%2039.5,more%20than%2070%20million%20people.

Adachi, Nobuko, guest editor, 2010. East Asian Transnational Migrants and Culture in a Global World. Encounters, fall.

Ana, Timothy, 2011. "The Genetic Diversity and Population History of Indigenous Peoples in Asia." Dissertation, Department of Genetics, School of Life Science, The Graduate University for Advanced Studies (SOKENDAI), date unknown. Accessed 17 February 2022 at https://core.ac.uk/display/148343440.

Arts, Bas, 2003. "Non-state Actors in Global Governance: Three Faces of Power." Preprints aus der Max-Planck-Projektgruppe Recht der Gemeinschaftsgüter, No. 2003/4, Max-Planck-Projektgruppe Recht der Gemeinschaftsgüter, Bonn. Accessed 31 January 2022 at https://www.econstor.eu/bitstream/10419/85112/1/2003-04_online.pdf.

Bellwood, Peter, James J. Fox, 1995. "The Austronesians: Historical and Comparative Perspectives." Accessed 7 February 2022 at https://press-files.anu.edu.au/downloads/press/p69411/mobile/index.html.

Bevir, Mark, ed. "Transnational Governance." In *Encyclopedia of Governance*. Accessed 12 March 2022 at https://sk.sagepub.com/reference/governance/n546.xml.

Biedermann, Reinhard, 2017. "Taiwan's Polycentric Strategy Within the Environmental Regime Complex on Climate Change." *ASIEN*, 143, April, S.

D. Pendery, *Transnational Taiwan*,
https://doi.org/10.1007/978-981-19-4368-3

25–46. Accessed 19 December 2021 at http://asienforschung.de/wp-content/uploads/2018/03/143_RA_Biedermann_ClimateChange_final.pdf.

Bourne, Randolph S., 1916. "Trans-national America." *The Atlantic*. Accessed 9 March 2022 at https://www.theatlantic.com/magazine/archive/1916/07/trans-national-america/304838/.

Britanica. "Transnationalism." Accessed 12 March 2022 at https://www.britannica.com/topic/transnationalism.

Chen, Estey, 2021. "Uneven Refugee Protections Across Southeast Asia Put Migrants at Risk." Accessed 21 March 2022 at https://www.csis.org/blogs/new-perspectives-asia/uneven-refugee-protections-across-southeast-asia-put-migrants-risk#:~:text=Southeast%20Asia%20hosted%202.1%20million%20forced%20migrants%20in,mechanism%20to%20coordinate%20policy%20responses%20to%20refugee%20populations.

Chen, Judy, 2021. "Coming Home to a Place I've Never Lived." *The News Lens*. Accessed 2 January 2022 at https://international.thenewslens.com/feature/taiwan-stories-of-return/151088.

Chen Yu-fu, Kayleigh Madjar, 2022. "Taiwan's Influence Growing, Despite China, Minister Says." *Taipei Times*, 3 May. Located at https://taipeitimes.com/News/taiwan/archives/2022/05/03/2003777630.

Clark, Greg, 2016. "How cities took over the world: A history of globalisation spanning 4,000 years." *The Guardian*. Located at https://www.theguardian.com/cities/2016/dec/01/how-cities-took-over-the-world-a-history-of-globalisation-spanning-4000-years.

Dahinden, Janine, 2009. "Are We All Transnationals Now? Network Transnationalism and Transnational Subjectivity: The Differing Impacts of Globalization on the Inhabitants of a Small Swiss City." *Ethnic and Racial Studies*, 32.8: 1365–1386. Accessed 7 February 2022 at https://www.tandfonline.com/doi/abs/10.1080/01419870802506534?journalCode=rers20.

Darrell Tryon Betsill, Michele M., Elisabeth Corell, 2008. "NGO Diplomacy: The Influence of Nongovernmental Organizations in International Environmental Negotiations." *Global Environmental Politics*, 8.4: 146–148. Accessed 14 November 2021 at https://www.researchgate.net/publication/23546964_NGO_Diplomacy_The_Influence_of_Nongovernmental_Organizations_in_International_Environmental_Negotiations.

Directorate-General of Budget, Accounting and Statistics, Executive Yuan, Republic of China, Taiwan, from personal communication with author.

Djelic, Marie-Laure, Kerstin Sahlin-Andersson, eds., 2006. *Transnational Governance: Institutional Dynamics of Regulation*. Cambridge UP.

Dobson, Kit, Date unknown. "Transnational Subjectivities: Roy Miki's Surrender and Global Displacements." Accessed 17 February 2022 at https://journals.lib.unb.ca/index.php/scl/article/view/10572/11158.

Dunn, Kevin M., 2005. "A Paradigm of Transnationalism for Migration Studies." *New Zealand Population Review*, 31.2: 15–31. © 2005 Population Association of New Zealand. Accessed 15 March 2022 at https://www.westernsydney.edu.au/__data/assets/pdf_file/0020/26633/A26.pdf.

Dupont, Alan, 2001. *East Asia Imperilled: Transnational Challenges to Security*. Cambridge UP. Accessed 21 February 2022 at https://books.google.com.tw/books. The entire Internet address is not included here and this book can be found at books.google.com.

European Commission. "Transnational Business Cooperation." Accessed 7 January 2022 at https://ec.europa.eu/growth/sectors/tourism/business-portal/internationalisation-tourism-businesses/transnational-business-cooperation_en.

Fang Tzu Chang, 2018. *somewhere we belong*. Translated by Charles Chen. Show Art Publishing.

Fichera, Massimo, Oreste Pollicino, 2019. "The Dialectics Between Constitutional Identity and Common Constitutional Traditions: Which Language for Cooperative Constitutionalism in Europe?" *German Law Journal*: 1097–1118. Cambridge UP. Accessed 31 January 2022 at https://www.cambridge.org/core/services/aop-cambridge-core/content/view/E8D1FE181EB6A389ED739155A8F3BB80/S2071832219000828a.pdf/the-dialectics-between-constitutional-identity-and-common-constitutional-traditions-which-language-for-cooperative-constitutionalism-in-europe.pdf.

Financial Supervisory Commission, Republic of China. "Taiwan's 2030 Goal to Become a Bilingual Nation." Accessed 17 April 2022 at https://www.fsc.gov.tw/en/home.jsp?id=253&parentpath=0,4,212,252.

Focus Taiwan, 16 December 2021. "Number of Taiwanese Working Overseas in 2020 Hits 11-Year Low." Accessed 12 January 2022 at https://focustaiwan.tw/business/202112160016.

Gill, Don Maclain, 2020. "The Role of Non-state Actors in Forging Closer India-Taiwan Relations." *Taiwan Insight*. Accessed 12 March 2022 at https://taiwaninsight.org/2020/10/20/the-role-of-non-state-actors-in-forging-closer-india-taiwan-relations/.

Global Trade Review (GTR), "EBRD to Work Together with Silk Road Fund." Located at https://www.gtreview.com/news/asia/ebrd-to-work-together-with-silk-road-fund/.

"Goodreads." Located at https://www.goodreads.com/.

Held, David, 1995. *Democracy and the Global Order: From the Modern State to Cosmopolitan Governance*. Stanford UP, © 1995 by David Held. Accessed 23 December 2021 at https://books.google.com.tw/books/about/Democracy_and_the_Global_Order.html?id=bkP4OVTlkjAC&redir_esc=y.

Held, David, Anthony McGrew, David Goldblatt, Jonathan Perraton, 1999. *Global Transformations: Politics, Economics, and Culture*. Polity Press.

Heylen, Ann 2010. "The Transnational in Taiwan History: A Preliminary Exploration." *Concentric: Literary and Cultural Studies*, 36.1, March: 9–33. Accessed 14 April 2022 at http://www.concentric-literature.url.tw/issues/Transnational%20Taiwan/2.pdf.

Hierlemann, Dominik, Stefan Roch, 2020. "Digital Participation in Taiwan: Takeaways for Europe." Published in *Participo.* Accessed 12 November 2021 at https://medium.com/participo/digital-participation-in-taiwan-8f5b020afbc4#:~:text=Digital%20tools%20for%20citizens%E2%80%99%20participation%20have%20become%20a,Taiwan%20began%20its%20transition%20from%20authoritarianism%20towards%20democracy.

Hsu, Caroline S., Kasin Tejapira, eds., 2001. *Traveling Nation-Makers: Transnational Flows and Movements in the Making of Modern Southeast Asia*. NUS Press, in association with Kyoto UP.

Hualien Indigenous Peoples Department. Accessed at various times at https://ab.hl.gov.tw/en-us/Home/Index.

Huang, S., 2009. "Transnationality: The Logics of Transnationality." In International Encyclopedia of Human Geography. Located at ScienceDirect, "Transnationalism." Accessed 10 March 2022 at https://www.sciencedirect.com/topics/social-sciences/transnationalism.

Hung Mei-hsiu, Kayleigh Madjar, with staff writer and CNA, 28 July 2022. *Taipei Times*, "Treasure trove of prehistoric tools found in Oluanpi." Locatedd at https://www.taipeitimes.com/News/taiwan/archives/2022/07/28/2003782567.

Huntington, Samuel P., 1996. *The Clash of Civilizations and the Remaking of World Order*. Simon and Schuster.

———, 2011. *Transnational Organizations in World Politics*. Cambridge UP.

Hussain, Dr. Irshad, 2007. "Transnational Education: Concept and Methods." *Turkish Online Journal of Distance Education*, 8.1, January: Article: 13. Accessed 15 February 2022 at https://files.eric.ed.gov/fulltext/ED494810.pdf.

International Organization for Migration, UN Migration. "Resettlement." Accessed 23 March 2022 at https://medialib.iom.int/galleries/browse/resettlement?content=any.

Jinam, Timothy adrian Anak Joseph, 2011. "The Genetic Diversity and Population History of Indigenous Peoples in Asia." Dissertation, Department of Genetics, School of Life Science, The Graduate University for Advanced Studies (SOKENDAI). Accessed 5 February 2022 at https://ir.soken.ac.jp/index.php?active_action=repository_view_main_item_detail&page_id=29&block_id=155&item_id=2706&item_no=1.

Kabinawa, Ratih, 2021. "Bringing Back Transnational Relations: Non-state Actors in Taiwan's New Southbound Policy." *Taiwan Insight*, 22 April.

Accessed 15 March 2022 at https://taiwaninsight.org/2021/04/22/bringing-back-transnational-relations-non-state-actors-in-taiwans-new-southbound-policy/.

Kissinger, Henry, 2014. *World Order: Reflections on the Character of Nations and the Course of History*. Penguin Books.

Knowledge Platform Security & Rule of Law, 2017. "Understanding Types of Transnational Conflict for Coherent Policy." Accessed 19 November 2021 at https://www.kpsrl.org/blog/understanding-types-of-transnational-conflict-for-coherent-policy.

Ko, Albert Min-Shan, Chung-Yu Chen, Qiaomei Fu, Frederick Delfin, Mingkun Li, Hung-Lin Chiu, Mark Stoneking, Ying-Chin Ko, 2014. "Early Austronesians: Into and Out of Taiwan." *American Journal of Human Genetics*, 94.3, March 6: 426–436. Accessed 10 March 2022 at https://www.ncbi.nlm.nih.gov/pmc/articles/PMC3951936/.

Kuo, Su-chiu, 2019. "New Frontiers in the Neolithic Archaeology of Taiwan (5600–1800 BP): A Perspective of Maritime Cultural Interaction." In *The Archaeology of Asia-Pacific Navigation*, Volume 3, Springer, Chunming Wu, Series Editor. Accessed 7 January 2022 at https://www.academia.edu/43631953/New_Frontiers_in_the_Neolithic_Archaeology_of_Taiwan_5600_1800_BP_A_Perspective_of_Maritime_Cultural_Interaction.

Ladurie, Emmanuel Le Roy, 1978. *Montaillou*. Penguin Books.

Liao, George, 2020. "Coca-Cola Launches Four Taiwan-Themed Bottles." *Taiwan News*. Accessed 5 March 2022 at https://www.taiwannews.com.tw/en/news/3949580.

Liew, Kai Khiun, 2016. *Transnational Memory and Popular Culture in East and Southeast Asia*. Rowman and Littlefield.

Lin, Arianna Fang-Yu, 2020. "Internationalization Initiatives of Taiwan's Higher Education: A Stepping Stone to Regional Talent Circulation or Reproduction of Unbalanced Mobility Scheme?" *Initiatives of Taiwan's Higher Education*, 69. Accessed 13 March 2022 at https://www.emerald.com/insight/content/doi/10.1108/HEED-06-2020-0017/full/pdf.

The LoadStar. "Taiwan Ports of Kaohsiung and Taipei Embraced by Silk Road Shipping Platform." Located at https://theloadstar.com/taiwan-ports-of-kaohsiung-and-taipei-embraced-by-silk-road-shipping-platform/.

Mao, Huan-wen, 2005. "Event Celebrates Seafaring Culture." *Taipei Times*, 4 August. Accessed 5 January 2022 at https://www.taipeitimes.com/News/taiwan/archives/2005/08/04/2003266339.

McIntosh, Matthew A., 2020. "Indigenous Navigation and Settlement of the Ancient Pacific." Accessed 12 December 2021 at https://brewminate.com/indigenous-navigation-and-settlement-of-the-ancient-pacific/.

Ministry of Education, Taiwan. "Higher Education SPROUT Project." Located at https://sprout.moe.edu.tw/SproutWeb/Home/Index/en.

———. "The Strategy of Taiwan Higher Education Internationalization." Accessed 22 January 2022 at https://www.fichet.org.tw/wp-content/uploads/2013/06/01%E5%B0%88%E9%A1%8C1_%E6%95%99%E8%82%B2%E9%83%A8%E6%9E%97%E6%96%87%E9%80%9A-%E5%8F%B8%E9%95%B7.pdf.

Mona, Awi, 2007. "International Perspective on the Constitutionality of Indigenous Peoples' Rights." *Taiwan International Studies Quarterly*, Summer, 3.2: 85–139. Accessed 21 February 2022 at http://tisanet.org/quarterly/3-2-4.pdf.

National Geographic TW. "Secrets of the Ocean Tribes." Accessed 7 January 2022 at https://www.youtube.com/watch?v=bC1H-UI57hE.

National Geographic Society. "The Silk Road." Accessed 3 March 2022 at https://www.nationalgeographic.org/encyclopedia/silk-road/.

O'Neil, Kevin, 2003. "Brain Drain and Gain: The Case of Taiwan." Migration Policy Institute. Accessed 2 March 2022 at https://www.migrationpolicy.org/article/brain-drain-and-gain-case-taiwan.

Paulus, Andreas, Mindia Vashakmadze, 2009. "Asymmetrical War and the Notion of Armed Conflict—A Tentative Conceptualization." *International Review of the Red Cross*, 91.873, March. Accessed 6 January 2022 at https://www.corteidh.or.cr/tablas/R23029.pdf.

Pendery, David, 2018. "Taiwanese Settling Far and Wide: A Global View." *Taipei Times*, 5 February. Located at https://www.taipeitimes.com/News/editorials/archives/2018/02/05/2003687071

———, 2019a. "Taiwan Is a True Transnational State." *Taipei Times*, 3 July. Located at https://www.taipeitimes.com/News/editorials/archives/2019/07/03/2003718013.

———, 2019b. "New Approach to Diplomatic Bind." *Taipei Times*, 6 October. Located at https://www.taipeitimes.com/News/editorials/archives/2019/10/06/2003723453.

———, 2019c. "Taiwan a 'City on a Hill' for Asia." *Taipei Times*, 2 April. Located at http://www.taipeitimes.com/News/editorials/archives/2019/04/02/2003712626.

———, 2020. *Taiwan—A Light in the East: A Personal and Analytical Taiwan Study*. Palgrave Macmillan.

———, 2022. "Taiwan Diplomacy: Worth the Effort?" *Taiwan Insight*. Taiwan Studies Programme at the University of Nottingham. 8 March. Located at https://taiwaninsight.org/2022/03/07/taiwan-diplomacy-worth-the-effort/.

Pieke, Frank N., Xiang Biao 2010. "Legality and Labor: Chinese Migratory Workers in Great Britain." In *Encounters: East Asian Transnational Migrants and Culture in a Global World*, Nobuko Adachi, guest editor, number 3, fall.

reliefweb, 2019. "Transnational Conflict in Africa (10 October 2019)." Located at https://reliefweb.int/report/world/transnational-conflict-africa-10-october-2019.

Reuters, 2 March 2022. "Taiwan President to Donate a Month's Salary for Ukraine Relief Efforts." Located at https://www.reuters.com/world/china/taiwan-president-donate-salary-ukraine-relief-efforts-2022-03-02/.

Robinson, William I., 1998. "Beyond Nation-State Paradigms: Globalization, Sociology, and the Challenge of Transnational Studies." *Sociological Forum*, 13.4.

Said, Edward W., 1993–1994. *Culture and Imperialism*. Vintage Books.

Science Daily, 27 January 2009. "Pacific People Spread from Taiwan, Language Evolution, Study Shows." Source, U of Auckland. Accessed 2 February 2022 at https://www.sciencedaily.com/releases/2009/01/090122141146.htm.

Smartling, "What Is a Transnational Strategy? + 5 Examples." Located at https://www.smartling.com/resources/101/what-is-a-transnational-strategy-5-examples/.

Smith, Michael Peter; Eduardo Guarnizo, eds., 1998. *Transnationalism From Below, Comparative Urban and Community Research*. Transaction Publishers. Accessed 25 December 2021 at https://books.google.com.tw/books/about/Transnationalism_from_Below.html?id=zTxYLmr7g_YC&redir_esc=y.

Sørensen, Ninna Nyberg 2007. "Living Across Worlds: Diaspora, Development and Transnational Engagement." International Organization for Migration.

Statista. "Number of Students from Taiwan Studying Abroad in Academic Year 2019/20, by Major Destination Countries." Accessed 22 March 2022 at https://www.statista.com/statistics/1092368/taiwan-students-studying-abroad-by-destination-country/.

Stewart. Ciloue Cheng, 2000. "Chinese American Families from Taiwan: A Transnational Study of Filial Connection." A doctoral thesis submitted to the faculty of the graduate school of the University of Minnesota.

Sun, Wanning, 2002. *Leaving China: Media, Migration, and Transnational Imagination*. Rowman and Littlefield Publishers. Accessed 15 March 2022 at https://books.google.com.tw/books/about/Leaving_China.html?id=xLmvgTnTYHwC&redir_esc=y.

Surot, Asan, 2022. Personal interview, Taipei, Taiwan, 28 March.

Taipei Times, unsigned editorial, 26 March 2022. "Taiwan Should Lead on Migrant Rights." Located at https://taipeitimes.com/News/editorials/archives/2022/03/26/2003775463.

Taipei Times, staff writer, 15 April 2022. "Taiwan to Send NCOs to US: Source." Located at https://www.taipeitimes.com/News/taiwan/archives/2022/04/15/2003776646.

Taiwan Asia Exchange Foundation (TAEF). Accessed 1 March 2022 at https://www.taef.org/about

Taiwan Council of Indigenous Peoples. "The Tribes in Taiwan." Accessed at various times at https://www.cip.gov.tw/en/tribe/grid-list/50AABE9D1284F664D0636733C6861689/info.html?cumid=5DD9C4959C302B9FD0636733C6861689.

Taiwan NextGen Foundation. "Empowering the Next Generation of Taiwan's Leaders." Accessed 15 March 2022 at https://en.taiwannextgenfoundation.org/about.

Taiwan News, staff reporter, 2005. "McDonald's Offering Rice Burgers." Located at https://www.taiwannews.com.tw/en/news/135948.

Taiwan Panorama. "The New Silk Road." Located at https://www.taiwan-panorama.com/en/Articles/Details?Guid=06fca070-7058-4840-bc67-98f39c267c84&CatId=9&postname=The%20New%20Silk%20Road.

Taiwan Today, 2021. "CIP Launches Book on Origins of the Austronesians." Accessed 28 March 2022 at https://nspp.mofa.gov.tw/nsppe/print.php?post=206280&unit=381.

Tang, Audrey, 2019. "Inside Taiwan's New Digital Democracy." *The Economist*. Accessed 21 February 2022 at https://www.economist.com/open-future/2019/03/12/inside-taiwans-new-digital-democracy.

Thoughtco. "What Is Transnationalism? Definition, Pros, and Cons." Located at https://www.thoughtco.com/what-is-transnationalism-definition-pros-and-cons-5073163.

Tosu, Sayun, 28 March 2022. Personal interview with employee at the Taiwan Council of Indigenous Peoples.

Toulmin, Stephen, 1992. *Cosmopolis: The Hidden Agenda of Moder*nity. U of Chicago P.

Tourism Bureau, Republic of China. "Festivals." Accessed 1 March 2022 at https://eng.taiwan.net.tw/m1.aspx?sNo=0029007.

United Nations Department of Economic and Social Affairs (UNDESA), Population Division (2020). "International Migration 2020 Highlights" (ST/ESA/SER.A/452). Accessed 21 March 2022 at https://www.un.org/development/desa/pd/sites/www.un.org.development.desa.pd/files/undesa_pd_2020_international_migration_highlights.pdf.

UN-ESCAP. "What Is Good Governance?" Accessed 17 February 2022 at http://www.gdrc.org/u-gov/escap-governance.htm.

UNESCO. "The Overseas Chinese: A Long History." Accessed 21 January 2022 at http://corteidh.or.cr.

Wang, Horng-luen, 2000. "National Reflections on National Imaginations in Taiwan." *Theory, Culture and Society*, 17.4: 93–117. Accessed 3 March 2022 at https://www.ios.sinica.edu.tw/people/personal/hlwang/hlwang2000-1.pdf.

Wang, Yi-chih, 2020. "Taiwan's McDonald's 2.0 Moving Fast-Food Upmarket." *CommonWealth Magazine*. Located at https://english.cw.com.tw/article/article.action?id=2768.

Wikipedia. A number of Wikipedia/English articles were consulted for this work, including "Cultural Trait," "Demographics of Taiwan," "Emigration from the United Sates," "International Student," "Orchid Island," "Outrigger boat," "Overseas Chinese," "Overseas Taiwanese," "Population Growth," "Taiwanese indigenous peoples," "Taiwanese people," "Transnationalism," "Transnational corporation," "Trans-Pacific Partnership," "List of political parties in Taiwan," and "Silk Road."

Xinhuanet. "Xi Focus-Quotable Quotes: Xi Jinping on Belt and Road Initiative." Accessed 5 March 2022 at http://www.xinhuanet.com/english/2020-09/07/c_139349475.htm.

Yahoo News, 2 March 2022. "Taiwan President Promises One Month's Salary to Aid Humanitarian Relief Efforts for Ukraine." Located at https://sg.news.yahoo.com/taiwan-president-promises-one-month-121939701.html.

Yeoh, Brenda S.A., Katie Willis, 2004. *State/Nation/Transnation: Perspectives on Transnationalism in the Asia-Pacific*. Routledge.

Index

D. Pendery, *Transnational Taiwan*,
https://doi.org/10.1007/978-981-19-4368-3

The manufacturer's authorised representative in the EU is Springer Nature Customer Service Centre GmbH, Europaplatz 3, 69115 Heidelberg, Germany. If you have any concerns regarding our products, please contact ProductSafety@springernature.com

Printed and bound by CPI Group (UK) Ltd, Croydon, CR0 4YY
30/09/2026
02225260-0011